CRYING IN COLORS

The Poemography Of A Man

BY: MICHAEL GUINN

Crying In Colors The Poemography of a Man

By: Michael Guinn

ISBN: 978-0-9843255-6-6

ISBN: 0-9843255-6-5

Catalogue Number: TX 5-822-182

Cool Side of Average—Guinn, Michael (9-2-03)

Cover Art by: Kramer Displayed At Left Coast Galleries
Cover Designed by: Michael Guinn
Cover Created by: Anelda Ballard

Photographs by: Michael Guinn, www.photobucket.com, www.zawaj.com and www.scfnw.org.

No part of this publication may be reproduced, except in the case of quotation for articles or reviews.

This cannot be stored in retrieval systems or transmitted in any form or by any means, electronic, mechanical or otherwise without permission from the publisher Jazzy Kitty Publishing. Published by Jazzy Kitty Greetings Marketing & Publishing, LLC (Jazzy Kitty Publishing). Using Microsoft and Adobe Software. Available for Worldwide distribution.

For information regarding permission, please contact:

Michael Guinn at (817) 412-3964

jordanmichaelg@yahoo.com

jordanmichaelg99@aol.com

www.mikeguinn.com

ACKNOWLEDMENTS

First of all praises to God for His blessings.

A heartfelt thanks to Mom, Dad and my brothers whom I love.
For Love, I thank Joyce and Jordan
For hope, I thank Gerald Johnson
For friendship, I thank Marisa E. Pryor
For faith, I thank Spoken Images and the Fort Worth National Poetry Slam Team
For Creativity, I thank the Zawadi Writers
For Wisdom I thank God and the Tarrant County Poetry Community
A special thanks to Lisa Charles of Images Theater Troupe
To Ms. Fran Thompson and her family
And the Sacramento Poetry Center

From my heart, a very special thanks to Ms. Litza Boden for her wonderful display of inspirational art. (Litza, I bow to your vision)

TABLE OF CONTENTS

INTRODUCTION	i
Step up and be a Man about It!	01
The Very Best of Michael Guinn	02
Crying in Colors	03
Remember	04
Wings	06
The Sparrow	07
I'm Coming	08
About Michael Guinn and His Fort Worth Poetry Slams	10
Somewhere Up There	12
The Boy with the Broken Smile	14
Quotes	16
Insignifiny	17
I'm Sorry	18
SPIT!	20
MOIST	21
Tapology: The Spirit of Tap	22
Momma's Reflection	24
Confessions of a Pedophile	25
Breathe	27
Shades of Blue	28
Mountain Too High	29

TABLE OF CONTENTS

Gallows and Heavens	30
Waterfalls	31
Pana-Remains	32
Fractions	34
Bless the Child (Children of Sudan)	35
"Wake Up"	36
Twenty One Pounds Ago	38
NIGGOLOGY	39
Is Poetry A Gimmick?	40
Never Meant to Hurt You	42
I'm Waiting on You Lord	44
Power to Power	47
Stolen From Africa	48
Heaven's Highway	49
I	50
Slipping Through Cracks	51
One	52
A Kiss	53
Stormy Moments	54
There.	55
Faith	56
If I Had One Wish	57

TABLE OF CONTENTS

Resume for Friendship 59
Stars are Writing Poetry 61
Boneless 62
On the Inside 64
If I'd Known 65
After Work Amnesia 66
I Still Follow 67
Don't Just Be All You Can, Be More! 68
The List 69
Hear Me…Free Me 70
Malcolm Jamal Warner and Mike Guinn 71
Black Words 72
Butterfly Kisses 73
They Speak Through Me 74
Violation. 76
A New Foundation 77
Keeper of My Sun 78
Gone in an Instant 79
Dandelions in the Wind 80
Death of Dreams 81
Chocolate Kisses 82
When a Man Cries 83

TABLE OF CONTENTS

Recognize 84
Fight 86
Benefit of the Doubt 87
In Your Eyes 88
Everyday 89
The Color of Freedom 90
Hold On 91
Shy Compliments 92
Guide to Becoming Real Men 93
Things Women Do/Things Men Do.. 94
You Should Have 95
That Rope 96
In My Son's Eyes 98
The Taste of Touch 99
I Thought of you Today 100
Heart of a Slave 102
What's that Sound? 104
My Color My Crime 105
The Basic of Chivalry 106
Greetings From Mike Guinn 107
Beautiful 108
Tribute 109
Hands of Time 110

TABLE OF CONTENTS

Daddy's Little Girl 111
Love Me Knots 113
Paralyzed 115
The Heart of a Man Who Screams 116
Little Winky 118
Bastard 119
A Poet 120
The Blackest Child 122
Where Souls Grow 123
Africa 125
Candlelight Reminds Me 126
We Miss You 127
Love's Jambalaya 128
On the Wings of Destiny 129
A Thousand Tomorrows. 130
That Island in Your Eyes 131
Mourning 132
Centric 133
In Our Heaven 134
Amazing Energy Photo's. 136
The Poetry of Change 137
Boo-Ku's 138

TABLE OF CONTENTS

Beginning of the End 139

Conversation with an Angel 140

Of Seasons Before 141

Without You 142

Shades of Day 143

A Stranger in Your Eyes 144

Shattered Glass 145

Through Ghetto Eyes 146

Blue Interludes 147

A Letter to My Brother 148

Shallow the Water 149

May I 150

An Angel's Halo 151

The Color of Misty Blues 152

Finding Your Own Voice 153

Sometimes we all Cry in Colors 155

Trails of Tears 156

Silhouette 158

INTRODUCTION

Michael Guinn was born in the small east Texas town of Jacksonville where he lived with his 4 brothers, Charles Jr., Maurice, Mark, and Derek. His mother and father were Mr. and Mrs. Charles and Evelene Guinn. His mother had 8 brothers; his father was the only child. Mom was raised in Cherokee county and did not finish high school. Father finished high school and played semi pro basketball and worked in construction. As long as I can remember my father has been a hustler. My mother, to this day, is still employed and always has worked at some job, whether it be construction, maid, housekeeper, care taker. Dad gave up on corporate America and engaged in a series of odd jobs. Chickens, Fire Wood, Scrap Metal etc..., all were a front for his real money maker—MARIJUANA. My family was as dysfunctional as they come.

My parents sent me packing at 13 to live with my grandmother, who had already suffered two strokes as a result of us bad ass kids. We had no structure and an abusive father who seemed to get off on how he "disciplined" us. Wire hangers, switches, extension cords were the norm.

At age nine, I suffered third degree burns to my arms, and since we had no insurance, I have scars, internally and externally.

I graduated from high school and enrolled in a small junior college in Ranger, Texas. There were more skunks than people and lots of racism. I left there the next semester and enrolled in Wharton Country Jr. College in Wharton, Texas. I ran track, pole vaulted, did well in high school, and excelled in college. After graduating from Wharton County, I received a scholarship to Lamar University in Beaumont.

There I lived with a girl named Felicia Albin Callous. She had rescued me from myself and was my first kiss, first uhhmm, well you know.

I left Lamar my senior year and enrolled in the U.S. Army and was stationed at Fort Jackson in Columbia SC. I met a girl named Susan Elece Sanders, who was another good woman I let, slip away.

I came home and went to work for Rusk State Mental Hospital in east Texas. I met Patty Johnson, the mother of my oldest son, Gerald, who is stationed in San Diego in the U.S. Navy.

Then I went back to school at Stephen F. Austin, met my son's mother there and graduated and went to work for CPS. I left east Texas and moved to Dallas where I began writing poetry. I started the Fort Worth Poetry Slams. And then after 6 years of CPS I left that job and Texas and moved to Sacramento. There I excelled in acting and spoken-word poetry slams. After being shot twice in an attempted carjacking, I moved back to Arlington and the rest of my story is woven in the poems you'll read in this book.

Enjoy my life's work and my life as a man struggling to be a MAN in a world of colorful distractions.

Welcome to Crying In Colors…The Poemography of A Man!

"I simply love the beautiful torment of a springtime tornado. It's desperate struggle to survive. The way it brutally spins itself in circles for acceptance not knowing that it's destroying lives trying to sustain its own. And I've never felt closer to Mother Nature than right now..."
:
Mike Guinn

Step up and be a
man about it!
No More Excuses
No more Lies
The Time is Now!

It's All On U!

For more info
Please visit…
www.mikeguinn.com

THE VERY BEST OF MICHAEL GUINN

CRYING IN COLORS

The Poemography Of A Man

Michael Guinn-MSW
Author-Activist-Motivational Specialist

Cover Art by Kramer Displayed At Left Coast Galleries
12324 Ventura Boulevard • Studio City, California 91604
818-760-7010 • Fax: 818-760-4164

http://www.leftcoastgalleries.com/artists/kramer-new/art/bmk_KramerCrying-48x48.htm

REMEMBER

Lil' Miss Poetry

I remember the winter you sent her.
An innocent infant meant to be sent.
And this…was as close as I'd ever come giving birth.
I remember!

She was left on the steps of my dreams, still wet from ink and screams…
Just a moment at the tip of my pen…so frightened and magnificent…then…
And I remember!

I fed her secrets, so she could survive my lies,
wrapped her in wisdom and stood by her side.
Laid her out on the page of my soul and watched her passion grow.
Listened to gurgles and giggles as she tickled the sheets with wiggles.

Watched her chase sonnets till sundown, play tag with life and old frowns.
And I just…smiled…"OH, SHE" was so young back then…
Temptation's timeless toddler. And I remember!

Her first words…were "I love you."
Spoke the native Haiku… and I never knew a child to smile that way…
Oh… how she shone like the sun that day.

I remember her first steps when we released her in a playground of freedom and leisure, as she wobbled up hills of drudgery, climbed mountains of recovery till she reached peaks of discovery. And once there, she perched high at the tip of summer, sprang forth from cliffs of wonder, till her voice became our thunder. Can't you hear her…?? I can...

She's as fidgety as ancient cousins, creating new discussions at a preschool of pronouns fussing…and I was so proud to behold her as I danced like a starving warrior, belly full of pride and hunger…And Oh how I loved her…then…
I Remember?

Together we must raise her questions and watch her young suggestions blossom into teenage confessions.

And as she grows…our sins turn gray on chins, from the things we did back then. When we didn't know any betta….And thought we'd live forever…

We won't, but she will.
She's the reflection in our menstrual mirror...without meaning no one hears her.
And if we'll just show her some appreciation…
For use of her annunciation…Maybe, just maybe she'll stay…

Wings

Written For Ms. Colleta Brown Sheppard

*High up in a clear blue sky,
I rise
Soaring in symphonies.
Gliding upon an orchestra of freedom.*

*Now as I fly, I take a deep breath and taste
the sun laughing in lemon drops.
While clouds smile, soft candy cotton upon my face
and this moment becomes the sweetest memory I've ever known.*

"Wings, don't fail me now"

*Heaven howls a rhapsody that
beckons the air beneath my wings
to be at my command forever.*

*Strong, bold breezes cool the aches of my feathers
ruffling them with melodies.
Killing them softly with wind songs.
Guiding me back home where I belong.*

*Somehow I have to find a way to tomorrow.
You see my destiny is waiting for me there.
Hiding behind whispers,
waiting between drum beats.
Caressing my essence with the sound of silence.*

*And as I spread these wings,
I'll cut like black thunder.*

*Slicing the sky.
Committing felonies against the wind
setting the night on fire.*

*And nothing will stop my flight,
for I plan on flying forever.
So wings, don't fail me now,
I'm almost home.*

The Sparrow

Inspired By The Prayer That Saved My Life On July 5, 2002

With excerpts from a poem by the Poetess "ADIAH"

I was fortune's abandoned child trying to capture rainbows in vanilla skies.

So used to following the pattern of her wind that I willingly gave in to sin.
"I've never felt so low."

I simply did not wish to go on without the love of my life.
My mind and soul were completely and utterly lost because I refused to put God first. And pain settled like dust on my heart, and nothing had the chance to breathe.

Night waves crashed into day shores, and my life spiraled downward into an ocean of despair. I was drowning inside.
But one day God sent a messenger.
Mother to moonlight, Sister to the sun
A bearer of blessed wisdom for a new beginning.

She placed her palm on my soul, and I cried the cry of the broken.

But it was from her prayer that I gained strength,
From her words that my spirit was revived.

She saved my life and helped me to realize that every passing moment is a chance to start anew.
That each morning is God's touch of grace.
Another opportunity to build a nest from his faith.
To chirp his poetic praises. To live for him.

And even though just a twinkle in the eye of the storm.
I too have a purpose………..To Fly.

"Now I stand here with ruffled wings on the battlefield of time.
My heart drips truth drops huddled in muddy puddles of predestined eternity.

Infinity beckons me to emerge from worldly trenches clinching faith-shields and fire-cast breastplates. My path is to defend the honor of Zion's heavenly gates."
I am the sparrow... called into the army of the ONE.

My journey has just begun.

(Thanks for sharing your wisdom and faith on that day Mrs. Atkinson)

I'm Coming

Awakened by the light
I emerge from the night that surrounds me and breathe for the very first time.
I stand not yet a man trying to understand that my lack of faith so soon shall pass.
"Listen" Could it be you Lord...knocking at my heart's closed door?

COULD IT BE YOU LORD?

Turning thunder into flashes of wonder wrapped in symphonies of bright sound
deep down inside where river flow and spirit thrives.

COULD IT BE YOU?

Pulling tears from eyes too blind to see, so full of night schemes that become day-dreams
never be seen by you or me, at least not in this lifetime.

I know you've been waiting for me to finally open my eyes
and behold the truth told in the rhythm of my soul.
And I know it must be hard for you to float there and watch me wade in waters as deep
and as distant as the Nile while I just stand here and shiver
because my soul has never known a river.

But something's happening to me now.
There's this constant churning, twisting of truth, wrapping itself inside me
like wild weeds and I need to embrace the place where this seed...scorches a
path hotter than the burning bush and is just as new as my love for you.

Someone, help me please!
Because I'm feeling the Holy Spirit for the first time
and I don't know what to do.
You touch me and I be a trustee of the flame.
This can't be, sometimes I catch me calling your name.

I'm Coming *(Continued)*

And it's at this moment that I...realize...life is just a metaphor for something bigger than the breath of being free.
So here I am Lord...
I'm Coming.
With empty arms, and devotion on my back...
I'm Coming.
With bright eyes and open heart, I'm following faith's tracks.
I'm Coming.
Here then there then back to black.
I'm coming Jesus.
I'm coming Saints.
I'm coming Savoir.
FATHER PLEASE!!!
If you are ready?
I'm coming for you.

ABOUT MICHAEL GUINN AND HIS FORT WORTH POETRY SLAMS

Michael is a Texas native who holds a Masters Degree in social work. What he witnessed as a caseworker for Child Protective Services "is what inspired him to begin writing poetry. "Since then he has become one of the nation's top advocates for social justice using the art of high-powered poetry and spoken-word performances for awareness. He has received national acclaim for highly interactive creative writing workshops.

BIO HIGHLIGHTS:

In 2007, Michael placed 7th at the National Poetry Slam Championships, won the AIPF Slam, and was the runner-up at the Arkansas Grand Slam. He is an Omaha Grand Slam Champion and has appeared in the highly successful Poetry and Pose Fashion show with Eva Pigford and Keke Wyatt. He and his teammates consistently rank among the top national and international poets since they began sharing their soul in 2002. The Fort Worth National Poetry Slam Team has been ranked as high as #3 in the country. Members of this incredible group of poets have placed or won awards at almost every level of performance poetry competitions. He has opened for Russell Simmons and Malcolm Jamal Warner.

He has been involved in the New Word Poetry, Akoben Word Festival, Austin International Poetry Festival, Toronto International Slam Championships, Arkansas Grand Slam and Bluebonnet Poetry Slam, just to name a few. Michael and other members of the team have performed all over the country and parts of Canada (Toronto Music Festival) and are some of the most sought after spoken-word artists in the nation.

Their dynamic delivery and energetic performances have put venues on the spoken-word map??? (Are you saying that because of your energetic performances the places where you have performed have become famous? If not, I am not sure what you are saying.) They've worked as lead actors as well as appeared on television, magazines, radio, and Internet e-zines globally.

The group host "The Workshop," a performance poetry workshop for therapy and emotional literacy. Michael Guinn's leadership has ignited the spoken-word community in the Dallas, Fort Worth area by continuously holding consistent and poet friendly open mics and competitions every week. Affectionately, and appropriately dubbed **ONE OF THE HARDEST WORKING POETS IN THE U.S.**

Michael is the leading performance poet and creative writing workshop facilitator in Texas. His vision has driven him to author more than ten poetry chapbooks and four spoken-word CD's. He is a teacher, social worker, motivational speaker, mentor, and a voice for all. Check out www.mikeguinn.com or email us at jordanmichaelg@yahoo.com. **For Booking, contact Michael at (817) 412-3964.** Visit www.facebook.com/mikeguinn1 and also www.myspace.com/mikeguinn1 www.twitter.com.

This volume of work is an unrequited
reflection of the joys and pains from life's
lessons and loves lost.

It is a journey from the corner of my soul to the bottom of my heart
through the corridors of my mind then back again.

I want to share the story of my life through
poetry & spoken word.

"Somewhere Up There"

A Voice From the Rubble of the WTC...Sept 21, 2001,"

Hello down there.... HELLO?
Out from the darkness, you called to me as you crawled to me.
Scratching a path of sadness with numb thumbs,
 as night ran from the dawn,
deep down inside, I waited for you to come.

I heard you fiercely digging, and I prayed with my last breath
for you to "HURRY"... SAVE ME... PLEASE!

But as misery moaned, sadness screamed,
granite and stone ground bone,
as twisted beams crushed dreams,
and all I wanted...was to simply go home.

Tired and weary my heart grew from the wait.
Wondering when and what would be my fate.
I watched the reaper grim, grin his reply
this was NOT the way I wanted to die.

But the air grew thin, chills moved like wind.
Fear shattered hope from the tremble within.
There was hardly any light, I could barely cope.

As walls around me collapsed...so did my hopes.
Still... I heard you...digging with all your might.
I heard you...working night, day and night.
I tried to hold on, I tried to fight.
But my spirit, weakened, crawled toward the light.

And you... may not have known this at the time...
But I listen as you cried out to the remains
of my trembling shadow.
You may not have known this then...
But a part of me felt you lift my lifeless body
from the rubble...and for a second...
My soul smiled.

"Somewhere Up There" *(Continued)*

You may not have realized it, but as
I took my final breath.

My spirit hugged yours, as I lay limp
in your arms, and it was at this moment…
INSIDE…I LET GO!!!

You may never know how it felt
when your hands gently closed my eyes for the last time.

Or how warm your tears felt to my soul as they dripped from your cheeks to mine.

I begged JESUS!! TO PLEASE…LET ME SPEAK!

And even though it was too late to save my broken body…
I wanted to thank you for allowing my spirit to be released
from the rocks and bricks that bound me.

And as my spirit fled that moment,
I wanted to thank you for the songs you sang as night fell.
Sifting through mud and blood must have surely been hell.
As you searched debris with only nightmares to tell.

It's ok…don't cry… I have to go now.
But I just wanted you to know that when I get to heaven.

I will ask God to appoint me as your guardian angel.
I just wanted you to know that!

And on that day…I'll be watching and waiting to give you the handshake and hug life denied me.
So until then take care my friend and I'll see you soon…

SOMEWHERE UP THERE

The Boy with the Broken Smile

Adam's Story

It was August 16, 1997 and hotter than hell, far from Heaven when Adam cried for the last time. Right now at this very moment, they're sounding the AMBER ALERT in Heaven. And for a man who spent a lifetime dancing with the devil. I have no rhythm. I've been off balance ever since. Imagine being dropped in the middle of I-35 during rush hour only to be run over again and again. Now imagine that's how it feels when a baby is shaken. Run over. It happens!

Every day hundreds of infants get caught up in this traffic jam of rage. Have you ever tried to revive a lifeless child? It's like holding a microphone without sound. And I haven't slept soundly in years. Keep hearing witnesses say they heard his mama yell, "Shut up, shut up, you little piece of spit!" Because "He wouldn't stop Crying." But that's what babies do, they Cry! But she couldn't stand it. So she put her hand over his mouth, gritted her teeth and shook him so hard, the saints had seizures and Jesus bit his tongue.

And we didn't need forensics to figure out the marks on his face were rug burns from being dragged across the living room floor. And we didn't need photos to remember images of his fractured skull where she'd slammed his head against the kitchen door. And Lord knows we've tried to forget seeing cracked ribs snapped like matchsticks, protruding from that baby's back. But we'll never forget that. Never! Can't you see him gasping, choking, and screaming for his life lying in a litter box dying from heartbreak! And all around him, pieces of shattered smiles lay scattered across the pee stained crib of his soul. The blue veins in his clinched fist became palm trees for ghost as he clutched a bloody baby rattle. And we wondered how the hell did he hold on to that?

All because he wouldn't stop crying, cause he had the nerve to be hungry, cause he wanted Huggies when being pampered was asking too much from a mother who… shook her baby and broke his smile. You see that's what happens when children never raised try to raise children. They break them.

"It must have fell off the bed," she said. IT! I looked at this girl and I just wanted to shake her. Because somewhere between the dirty clothes and spoiled milk. Between the used condoms and cockroaches. Love lost its way.

Now I know it isn't a pretty picture but it has a purpose. Awareness for you - therapy for me. This is why we write—To motivate new voices to share their own story. No matter how sad. Now, it's not easy! But if you'll just climb down from the mountain inside, you too can write lullabies for the child with the broken smile.

That baby is in a safe place now. Where Martin is holding Coretta's hand again…Where children don't have to play double-dutch with the lightening of striking fists. Where there are no more sad stories from old poets with heavy hearts on a night when numbers don't mean nothing. And right now, I'm begging you to be more. Who is with me? Who else is brave enough, NO! Poet enough to stand here and actually use your gift for what God gave it to you for? To inspire, to teach, to save lives. Will it be you? YOU! Please tell me YOUR'E NEXT! Because there are angels sitting all around us, watching, making damn sure we get it right tonight. So that there'll be no more broken smiles. POETS-Our Children, are waiting for you.

Quotes

"I have a dream that one day, my father's fears, my mother's tears won't drown in the screams of forgotten years. And tomorrow's sun reappears with the dawn that rises here."

Michael Guinn

"Before attempting to comb through hairs of Wisdom, one must first massage the scalp with Knowledge."

Michael Guinn

Cover By Michael Guinn
Art Design By Ms. Litza Boden
Photos from Various Artists via Web.

Copyright 2003 Mental Massages Press
Michael Guinn– President/CEO
All Rights Reserved

Insignifiny

Passing by me...life denies my entrance
to a place where grinning sketches itch in skits,
Un-fetched reflections go matched,
and my surface is barely scratched.

Still time pauses long enough
for my essence to be captured by its light.
Smoothly transforming me into rhapsody
and my existence becomes crystal clear.

Now restless moments pace with nowhere to go,
caught up in contemplation,
confined between chalked outlines,
wandering between now and then.

It's in this instance that I realize...
That I am simply a missing link in evolution,
an epiphany of nothing....just a moment lost in time.

I'M SORRY
A Poetic Apology by Michael Guinn

Woman don't you know that I would give my soul to hold the mold God used to create your smile? And even though your winds spin like hurricanes within, it's still the closest to heaven I've ever been. And someday I'll write a poem that wins the Nobel peace prize for the peace I couldn't find in your eyes.

You…be that poet, writer, soul survivor and your misery cuts through me truly.
Taking me back to that moment in your story where you first lost your glory.
And I can only imagine how it must feel to have wings and not be able to fly.
That has to be the most painful feeling any woman could bear.
Well, I've never known that feeling. I've never felt the sting of words without wings become dirty pretty things.
And I've never screamed at the top of my lungs and had no one hear my cry.
I've never known what that was like ladies. I've never known.
And even though I've never been where you are, I can still feel the scar on your spirit. Cause when you speak…I hear it.
And even though I've never had hopes bashed.
I can still hear the echo of dreams smashed like a thousand fists against the windows of your past.

But I have had words trapped like Rosa Parks's verbs…dying to get out and had doubt just beat them back down until they became poetic lumps in the throat of my soul.
And I've waited a lifetime to fall in love, to be a part and had no one to share my heart.
I've know what that was like fellas!   I've known!

But today I **REFUSE** to let any woman stand there all alone wrapped in blues, clutching black, seeing red. YOUR VOICE WILL NOT BECOME SIGN LANGUAGE FOR THE GHOST OF YOUR ANGUISH! BECAUSE TODAY! YOUR …WORDS TAKE FLIGHT! THEY SOAR!

Traveling from metaphor to metaphor, giving life to incomplete sentences. THEY SOAR! Stretching the limitations of sound, your words fan the clouds and cool the sky. They Soar…Capturing the moment. They Soar!... Freeing the soul. They Soar! THEY SOAR!   And right now... I just wanna say. I'm sorry.

Sorry for every man who never said HE was sorry.
Sorry for all those times your essence was left dying in the shade of never...
Forever road kill for vultures who were too stupid to see that in your eyes blooms the seed of their culture. Sorry! For all those nights your heart was left tangled in the curve of a smile as crooked as his shifty grin. To me, THAT is the greatest sin!
And I want you to know that the prize you have inside could never match the beauty inside your eyes because you are **beautiful.**

And I promise. I PROMISE! To never disrespect you with my fist, hits or kicks.
Just protect you with love, wisdom, and my last wish…
And I know you may not believe me, I know But …Today…I'll take that chance to say...
LADIES! I AM SORRY!

SPIT!

Please Join DFW's #1 Spoken-word Promoter, Mr. Mike Guinn.

Every Sunday night to listen to the hottest online spoken-word radio show in Texas!

To Listen and be heard all over the world just call 646 595 4685 or log on to www.kebnradio.com

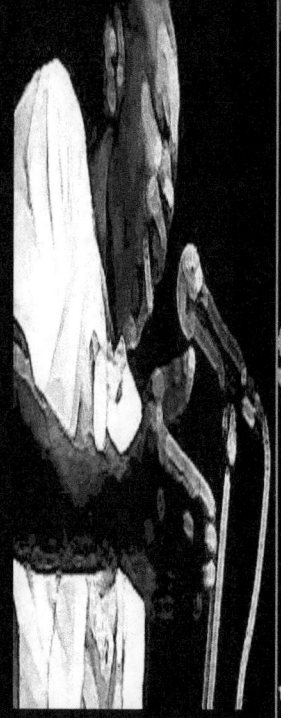

MIKE GUINN

SPIT!

Spoken word & Poetry In Texas

Listen Live ..

EVERY Sunday Night 8 - 10pm (CST) only at

www.KEBNRadio.com

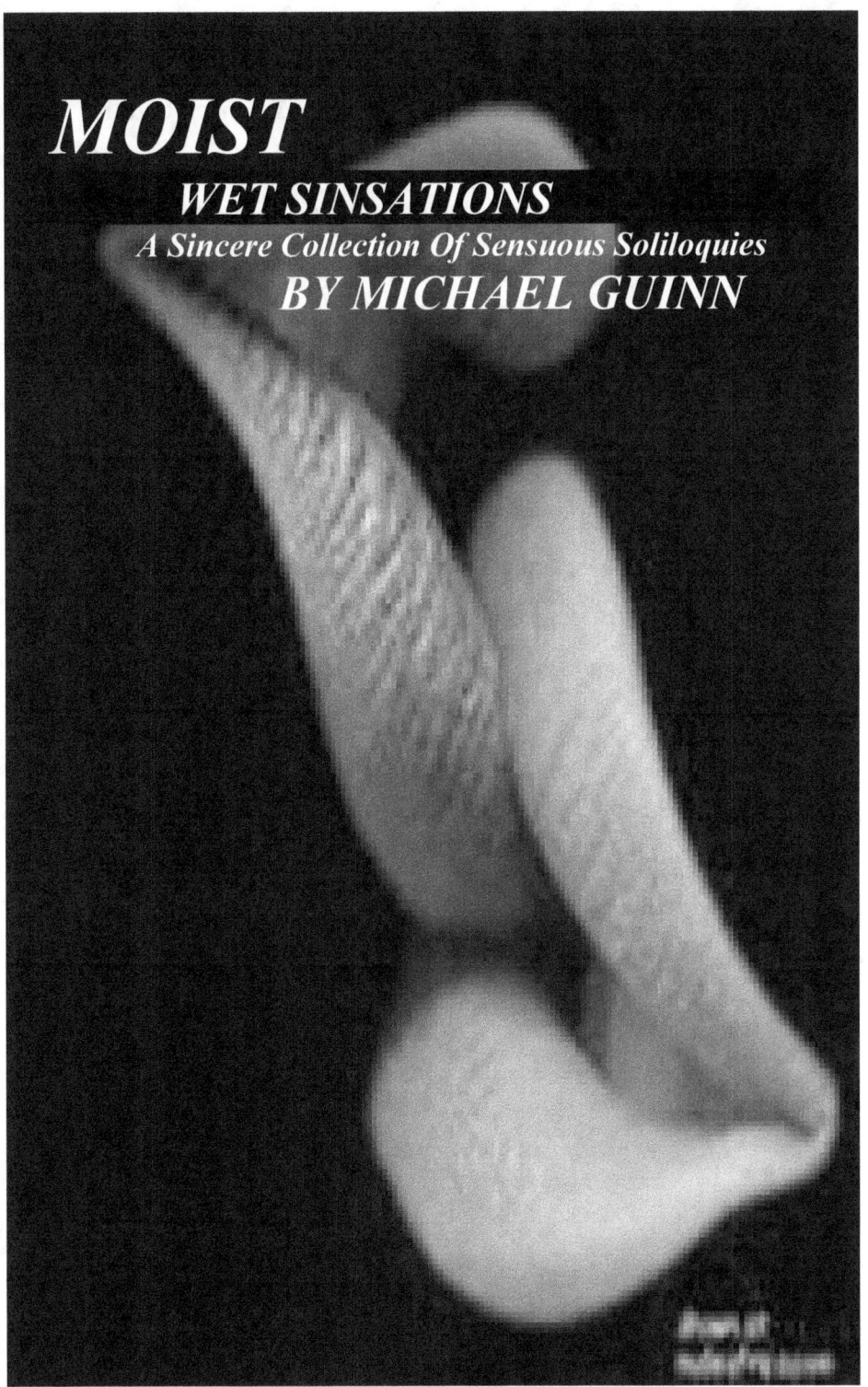

MOIST
WET SINSATIONS
A Sincere Collection Of Sensuous Soliloquies
BY MICHAEL GUINN

TAPOLOGY: THE SPIRIT OF TAP

Tap is more than just a fancy dance form. It's an American tradition that's evolved over a period of some three hundred years. Tap is a multicultural fusion of unbridled percussion deeply ingrained into the roots of our culture. It began as a mixture of soulful syncopation fueled by energy so passionate that even drums succumbed to its rhythm. A rhythm bursting from the soles of feet that wove powerful tapestries of jubilation and inspiration.

Tap told a story. Not with words... but with motion. It was a melting pot of performance enhanced dialect. A beautifully unique execution of sounds sent straight from the soul. From Irish moves to African grooves, tap gave us hope, brought us together, and bridged gaps with a language all its own.

There was no fancy choreography, no diagrams, or notes or anything to clog the imagination. Just a mountain jig of emotion corralled in multi-colored moments of improvisational artistry. Shoot...most tap dancers don't even know what they gon' do until they do it.

You see tap was more than just fast flashy combinations of high kicks or soft shoed melodies made up from the sticks...it was "The Dance of Angels."

The dedication to delivery, the butterfly brilliance, the bubbled perfection was in "Hines-sight." The single most authentic and significant melding of cultures in the world.

It was a vehicle for creative self-expression. And from this drive, this desire to express oneself, folks began to understand, appreciate and respect not just the art but the heart of one another. Tap transcended racism ya'll! It was one of the few times where no one could deny the talent, raw energy or SOUL of the performer no matter what their color.

Whether it was the sparkle of Shirley's swirl or hoofers heard around the world. The jazz of Honi Coles or the rhythm of Eleanor's stroll. Tap was simply magic!

From Fagan to Five Points, from Paradise Square to Philadelphia.
From Vaudeville to Sullivan, from Harlem to Hollywood.
From the plantation mud to the Cotton Club, from flips through the air to the grace of Fred Astaire. Tap was no ordinary form of entertainment. Tap was and always will be the timeless temple where dance was born.

Now I know some folk will try to deny the shuffle and sham of tap dancers who've stepped with angelic flair into history. But no one, I mean NO ONE will deny the boldness and pure energy of the artists and styles from that day still being performed to this one. This is their legacy and on this stage tonight, they give it to you. Each portrayal is created to chronicle the colorful and creative contributions that have invigorated the tap dance movement for hundreds of years.

So, tonight you'll hear and bear witness to some of the most amazing taps ever performed. From Bojangle's bold beats to Peg leg's defying feats, you will be transformed...as we share our soles through the Legends Of TAP!

"Momma's Reflection"

Two in the morning when "Momma" came home.
Opened the door to find her daughter's not alone.
Came in early, momma did, from the late night shift.
Saw daughter on the floor, two men standing stiff.

That moment, forever frozen in time.
If she could just find the button she'd hit rewind.
Her child stunned dem boys run.
Cause Momma interrupted their late night fun.

Hands on hips, daughter grins, and no attempt to deny.
No shame in her game, she smiles and says HI!
16 and mean, no love, no affection.
Momma saw herself in her daughter's reflection.

She thought about times she let things slip.
Talks and time-outs is how she lost her grip!
This was just daughter's way of having some fun.
She was only doing what Momma, had done.

So, don't blame her Momma, for things she do.
She was only acting just like you.
Next time think twice before you preach.
Cause the way you live is the lesson you teach.

CONFESSIONS OF A PEDOPHILE

It was a rainy day in May 2002, and I was to interview an ex con named Jessie. Now, just a few days after his release, we received a report about a little girl left naked in a cornfield near MLK. It was the case no one wanted, not even me. I was assigned because of my instinct and ability to get perverts to loosen up enough to tell the story. First question, "DID YOU DO IT JESSIE!" "NAW Man!"

But what his lips wouldn't speak, his eyes couldn't hide, and I had this feeling. I told him that little girl would never have children, never see out her right eye. SHE WOULD NEVER be the same.
My hands sweated as I gave stats on suicides and sex crimes and this time, I said "I know you did it Jessie, so just tell the damn story." These were his words.

About a year before I got out of prison, my uncle promised me a job driving a snow-cone truck. Now every day I would drive by that school playing the pedophile national anthem. POP GOES THE WEASEL! Made me feel like puberty's pied piper.

Then I saw her. 4 foot 2, skirt blue oooo... So I gave her extra stuff. You know the old pervert's courtship until I knew I had her...One day I waited till she got half way home from school and drove up beside her. Turned off my music and turned on the charm. Told her I had something special for her. She got in, I locked the door and got out of site. By then I was so damn horny, and she was wearing the victim's uniform. You know that white shirt, blue skirt they wear in middle school and I needed some real bad. See there's something special about that petite shape, cute face that's so sexy, especially when they're around 11 or 12. But as I raised her skirt to pull down her panties. She turned to me and said... "MY GRANDPA DOES THIS ON WEEKENDS; HE PLAYS WITH ME THIS

WAY!" Damn I thought she was fresh but it turns out she was just sloppy seconds and that pissed me off.

So I jabbed in one-two fingers and do you know that little tease didn't even squirm. And then I beat her till she bled blood clots and then I...Jessie stopped and stared as my hands slowly turned to fists.

WHY DID YOU DO THAT JESSIE? WHY? He said I can't help it...And as soon as I get out of prison, I'll probably do it again. Then he just grinned. I knew I was supposed to be professional, I knew I was supposed to go by the book... but what would you do? Then I snapped. Started thinking about my little girl. Kept seeing those ants crawl from her bloody thighs, so I beat his ass for every nipple he kissed, for all those little girls he made touch his filthy stick. And then I tried to jab my pencil up his ass for all.

What if she were your daughter or yours... Wouldn't you do what I did? POP GOES THE WEASEL BITCH! It took 2 co-workers, a security guards and a janitor to pull me off his ass. I broke down and cried because for the first time in my life, I WAS HUMAN. Her name was Maria. She committed suicide at sixteen. Her hands still tug at the sleeve of my soul every time I pick up a pen. I looked down at my fist, his face and my supervisor and said. YOU AIN'T GOT TO FIRE ME TODAY!
I QUIT!

Breathe

Spoken Images linger like echoes in the sand and
tiny little verbs run scared from the corners of my imagination.
  Where light becomes a warrior.
   Slinging syllables… at the wind,
    and my brothas strangle while struggling to hear the piercing
    scream of vicious words.

   But no one understands what I'm saying.
    Dead poets cry as they listen.
     Twisting in old coffins to get a better seat.
     Watching history as life retreats and while dark moments pace
     back and forth and back and forth.
      Time splits into halves and the day chases my meaning away.

      Still these vowels betray me now,
       like good brothas in disguise.
        Spitting haiku lies.
         Cradling metaphors without sun
         and these words become words,
         no one has ever heard.

    Now time sweats in minutes.
     Minutes that slither like snakes.
     But this poetry is in my system,
      and now is too late… I'm hooked.
       I've been addicted since the age of day.
       And these words be calling me… calling me
       Telling me to Freeze "brotha" freeze.
       Get off your knees brotha please.
        Relax… Open your mouth release,
         and just breathe.

   Breathe!
    So that these children understand your rhythm.
    Breathe!
     So that ropes no longer strangle moments
      that unravel into seconds divided by time

      Just breathe and go be that word warrior.
       Just breathe and go be that poet spinning
        verbs that define words that define worlds.
        Just run, jump, and breathe.
         Just hide, seek, and breathe.
         Just breathe, conceive, believe.
         Just open—release—breathe!
          Open—release—breathe!
         Breathe my brotha, breathe.
          So that when others feel that need…
         All they have to do is just   Breathe!

Shades of Blue

My mother, earth
   My father, time
      Brother winds
         Sister rains inside my mind
            Their frown, my moon, their smile, my sun
               Here together we live, together as one

            I've been dreaming in shades of blue again
              Misty colored memories crystallize upon my cheeks
            Like diamonds in the rough
            And hope becomes a collage of cold moods
         I'm dreaming in shades of blue

So strange mankind
    Painted in tints of summer shadows
       Tethered by winter gray shades of torment
          Spewing hate like crimson vines
              While precious seconds become insects eating away at time

            The elimination of my imagination
            Visions and interpretations
            Cause me to cry in colors
            Because we're still unable to love one another
            And the sting of tear drops stain as life becomes smothered

But these words are just words
    Defined by Words that Curse Words
       Confined in an evolution of time
          Revolving in an revolution of sound
             Evolving in an evolution of moods

And we are left dreaming in shades of blue.

Mountain Too High

A Ghetto Villanelle

I'm still standing and I don't know why.
The hill has become too rocky and my words refuse to climb.
Martin, please forgive me, but the mountain is too high.

The ancestors, they are screaming fly, boy, FLY!
But for their words, I have no answer.
I'm still standing and I don't know why.

I watch grandma kiss the sky.
I stumble, fall then crawl.
Martin, please forgive me, but the mountain is too high.

If my brothers offer no reply.
Then how can I begin my climb?
I'm still standing and I don't know why.

My sister's load is heavy; you can see it in her eyes.
Her back is much too fragile, her spirit is just too shy.
Martin, please forgive me, but the mountain is too high.

My mother's weeping legend, my father's dreams defy.
I have no one to help me, but me, myself, and I.
I'm still standing and I don't know why.
Martin, please forgive me, but the mountain is too high!

Gallows and Heavens

There are brothers still hangin'
in the gallows of our minds,
black and blue from the neck up.
Wearing loose nooses
like proud pieces of cheap jewelry.
Bling blinging. While swinging
to the rhythm of old negroes pickin' cotton.

"Swing low... sweet chariot"
Those brothers are still swinging where time forgot.

So foul this place where dreams make haste
and curious fruits sway to and fro
on pendulums of bare emotions.
And families lacking a strong black voice
become devoid of soulful sound,
speak in bogus lingo,
create tricky gestures with smooth hands.
Just happy to wear nappy roots
but can't comb through.
Look.!! Your brothers still swinging, their eyes are on you.

Inside this mental plantation,
third eye patches are worn like Heaven badges
covering old scars still oozing pus from unjust revolutions.

Dreams, what damn dreams?
Ain't no dreams when memories turn to dust.
Cotton becomes a fabric of twisted lies.
And hope is left scattered in empty fields
where death first sprouted.
Go ahead Sing... My brotha... Sing!!
"Swing low... sweet chariot."
......But our brothers are still swinging where time..

forgot

Waterfalls

Somewhere near by destiny
There's a book bubbling with black power
Haikus float on lily pads
As waterfalls rage with clarify

Sonnets shimmer like rainbows over rivers
As their spectrum separated the night
Thunder creates trembles and shivers
Splitting Sadness with its night

"Listen"

Gwendolyn is crying in colors again
Creating poetry in the image of my reflection

"Listen"
To splash of a million of tears
Trickling down ebony cheeks
Like spiraling Negro anthems

And like black rain
Time showers day with memories
Leaving year prints upon my face of my future

"Listen"
It's
Flowing

"Freedom"

PANA-REMAINS

She was a phenomenal woman....but she's gone... She told me she needed to see where she wanted to be... and Right Now I feel as helpless as an abandoned child in the middle of I-30 during rush hour dodging little silver Hondas switching lanes on their way to hotter springs.

I can't eat. I can't even sleep; all I can do is roll over and hope that life slows down long enough for me to learn to walk again.

But how can a man be strong when all along what he thought was right was wrong? How can someone just start a fire, without fanning the flames and then abandon a burning desire? GOD... you tell me how could you let them do that... to a good man. Tell me how can a heart so empty be so damn heavy?
So heavy that it cuts off the circulation to veins, killing membranes with strains that link into chains of pain... and all that's left are just
"PANA—REMAINS"

Oh, I've tried a little bit of everything. Aroma therapy... but all I could smell was her. Art appreciation only reminded me that in her eyes my value had depreciated. Tried alcohol... but you can only drink so much Riunite Lambrusco Before drowning in sorrow. Because without her there was no tomorrow.

And that ...that unbearable silence where once were the beat off two hearts, slowly smothers me. I'm choking. I can't breathe because what I thought I needed I could no longer have... at least not in this lifetime.

If only I'd seen the signs or had some training on how to recognize love's disguise. Somebody please tell me what good is my Master's Degree when I can't even master... me?

I'm trying to be a man tonight... Lord knows I am.

But I'd be lying if I said it didn't hurt…and I've already cried a river LANGSTON.
Because I was dying inside. And I'm still dying.

If only she'd stayed around long enough to see her seeds sprout spirit leaves, bearing
love's fruit on these life-limbs. If she'd just talked to me and told me what she truly
needed. I would've done anything. I would've sold my soul
because I loved her more than everlasting life. I just wanted to give her my all.
But it's alright because I'll live and learn to hold my head up again.

Learn to like myself and for the very first time I learn to love me just the way that I
am… even if I am without her.

But that night was the night the poetry almost died. Taking with it a part of my desire
that I was barely able to recover. That's why I didn't write for awhile. Because you
have to have a love for what you do in order to keep on doing it.
I guess that's why she left. For now… this is all that remains of my heart.

Fractions

Spoken images linger like echoes in the sand
While greatness becomes invisible to those
Whose thoughts wander like naked reminders of yesterday's sorrow
Despair cast shadows of then in shades of now
As Heaven legions curse that which refuses to breathe life into souls rotting from cultural decay

And while we fight like thieves for a single breeze
Old African spirits dance around a bonfire of whispers
Their reflection, becomes a drum beating thunder
...into an ocean of mirrors, as ignorant lips spit ill conceived notions into innocent eyes blinded by the walking dead

Confused with insanity, profanity slices the night
As chills rally in gleeful communion on angry black backs
Like teeth-prints etched on dark-skinned canvases
Death.... simply delights from the creation of a masterpiece

Our young, little soldiers of none
Become mesmerized by lies smoked in pipes, but see no peace
Instead they gather to play tag with bitter memories
Chase broken promises like Frisbees in the sky
Screaming at history, wondering why

"But wait," we've got yesterday in our pocket
Last night on our breath
Memories gathering dust on shelves of our self
And we be that still-born earth, fresh from God's own breath

He's standing at the door step, waiting to rush
While empty eyes remain shut from the guilt of sin
Death crawls in whispers, we die in vain
And a fraction of our history, is all that remain

Bless the Child

(Children of Sudan)

Fragile shanties fail to shelter hope beseeched by requiems
of far gone conclusions. As steady chants resound in sad lament,
confounding reality with truth's despair.

Harmony, is just a fairytale defiled by the stench of time.
In hungry minds whose sun refuses to shine.

Peace be not still, for my brother's children suffer
from the sickness of certain uncertainty, while they squint from
shadows of lifeless trees, where buried deep are the seeds of you and me.

Who will hold the child who weeps in their sleep with teeth?
Turning brown shades from the stain of cockroach suppers?

Who will hold the young whose tongues have already become raw
from sucking on bitter memories, as life-knots restrict the spoken image
of future glory.

Someone please, tell me who?

And as smiles fight through layers of dirty disappointments, tears form
mud puddles upon brown cheeks while pity pools create heartbreak in
eyes that cry out for hope.

Who will hold the child and give them back that smile?
Who will bless the child tonight?

Who will bless the child?

"Wake Up"

Last night, I was awaken from deep sleep, in cold sweats...shivering from a nightmare.

Now in this nightmare, I kept hearing the voice of Martin Luther say, "Free at Last." "Free at Last."

But for some reason, I found it difficult to listen to the wisdom of dead voices. Voices of revelations from revolutionary dead poets speaking eternally from eternity, as they angrily twist and turn in unmarked graves covered by shallow sands of time. And I wondered, "Was I that black assassin??

Did I silence that brotha's beating drum?"

Creating Queens of denial Emperors of none?

Not Me! You see, in this nightmare!

I seem to be too busy struggling to decipher untranslatable hieroglyphic scribbles of too much ... too little. While the haves sat un-moved.

Plotting, scheming, planting their little seeds of bogus hocus-pocus. Making me feel like some illiterate joker because I refuse to listen to un-written rules of injustice. And now confused swarms of Africanized bees, build hives that thrive on the limbs of weak family trees

The sting of honey vipers, milk money snipers wearing Hilfiger

Pulling triggers on other brothas in Hilfiger

Ambushing ripe fruits with ear shots. Wounding dreams as futures rot And while the moans and screams of bloody tomorrows drown out the sound of "FREE AT LAST"... rigamortus eclipses millennium's shadow. But time's shadows are already here YALL. Following close on the heels of forever, but we don't have forever to catch forever nor will we ever. All we got is what we get when fed BS in steady doses, comatose injected like infected fat rats in labs, turning lives into rehabs. Then Malcolm reached out to me. He said, "Here son ... take my hand grab it." GRAB IT.

"Wake Up" *(Continued)*

*Grad it and don't let go because letting go is a habit.
A habit of fear because our forefathers aren't here. But where's my father?
Where's my father, when I need him to teach me, to be me, the man I could be but
can't be because I can't see in front of me? So I keep slipping, falling, begging,
crawling through cracks of insanity praying this can't be.
Blue and black-eyed witnesses for years of mother's tears as sisters cry
and brothas die. While bullets fly and blood dries letting lifetimes pass us by.
And all we seem to do is chase moonbeams in mainstreams of hate, killing hope
in its wake. But wait! Wake up! Start "loving" one another. Wake up!
Help your sistah and brotha.
Wake up! "Please" WAKE UP!!*

Twenty One Pounds Ago

Only God knows or cares what happens when I walk out that door.

All I know is…

21 pounds ago, I was happy
Now I'm just a sad bag of confusion.
Losing my mind, trying to figga whether
I should pull the trigga on my reality.

Let the devil take my soul,
21 pounds ago TODAY, I LOST CONTROL.

There are memories that still haunt me.
Hell nobody sane wants me.
The scars from love and war,
just aren't becoming.

My perception of her deception is a reflection of my faith.
I have none, just a sun that sets way too late.

My definition of God's wisdom is a jaded cataclysm.
A faded inscription, man's depiction of some old time religion.

Sometimes I believe living is overrated.
21 pounds ago TONIGHT MY SPIRIT MIGHT HAVE MADE IT.

You see there is no hope in my future.
Just a heart full of sutures.
Patches of then, way back when
I didn't feel like such a loser.

So if this sounds like good-bye,
then baby, so shall it be.

21 pounds ago tomorrow
there was a poet
And I was HE.

NIGGOLOGY

Raging Blackness consumes me
It confuses my muse with melted black jazz
I don't know why
And I never thought to ask

But what I do know is…
With this creation of words, I'm on the verge
My verbs disperse as emotions submerge
My rhythm is cursed, my momentum disturbed
My voice is silent, my dreams deferred

While running on empty my mistakes follow me
My spirit gets lost in foolish ideology
If I could just stand, be a man, and stop making apologies
Then my anthology would be more than a history of "NIGGOLOGY"

Listen, there has to be a reason for wasted wishes
Broken broomstick reminders of hate's little kisses
Death follows me close chasing with switches
With my heart defeated, my future lies in stitches

"LISTEN"
I hear the ancestors screaming at my soul
YOU BETTA RUN SON, YOU BETTA RUN

Somehow I've got to break free before it's too late
I've got to stay strong and make my escape
Hate binds me, confines me, deep down inside me
No hope, I can't cope and the mirror reminds me
That YOU BETTA RUN SON, YOU BETTA RUN

But while shaving I began raving, my thoughts behaving
cutting edges between verbs from the words I'm saying
Slick Incantations curse my translations
The fire, hot, burns down my black nation

Now reflections of sins speak in tongues again
Restricted from me, my will gives in
This diseased striptease steals moments like thieves
On bloody knees, I'm begging get out of me please

Lord, I wish this hate would just leave me be
Somehow I've got to find a way to get this "NIGGA" out of me

IS POETRY A GIMMICK?
DO NIGHT CLUBS PIMP THE POETRY VIBE FOR PROFIT?
A NATIONWIDE PIMPEDEMIC! By Michael Guinn-www.mikeguinn.com

This article's primary purpose is to provoke thought and elicit feedback from poetry lovers and spoken-word enthusiast, Slam Teams and Touring Poets as well as all the literary folks and most of all promoters and host. Hopefully, this will create positive dialogue that elevates the appreciation of this art form and how it should be perceived by a whole new audience. Again, this article is not an attack on night clubs and should be seen as a point of discussion by those who make a living or aspire to make a living as a full or part-time poet or spoken-word artist. It's time to ask questions. This is only the first. Let the discussion begin.

What if you are a new or old poet who has spent painstaking hours crafting what you think is the perfect poem?

You re-write, rehearse and revise it over and over again until you believe it to be...pure art. You are proud of it, so proud in fact that you want to go share it with the world!

So you begin looking for places hoping that it is a place that embraces the passion and pure art of your poetic self-expression. So you search newspapers and the Internet, and then you come across a flyer that advertises poetry, comedy and karaoke with a live band to boot. Usually an event like this is hosted by some comedian or radio personality or someone in a certain poetry clique whose primary concern is for a pay check and could not care less about the quality of the environment let alone the historical ramifications of having poetry in that environment or the quality of work done by those poets.

That poet, unfortunately, is only a pawn, a filler for the real

entertainment which is the comedian, the music/band, ladies, and the drinks. So you go with the assumption that this might be a place where you could perform, share, and be embraced and appreciated by an AUDIENCE THAT APPRECIATES THE
ESSENCE OF THE ART THAT IS POETRY.

But you quickly discover that the fancy flyer, radio hype, and all the glitz are just a bunch of BS, and that they could not care less about your art. And the venue usually ends up being some smoky overcrowded, overpriced night club whose patron's main goal is to come drink, get high, or laid and whose management has been persuaded that they can get large crowds if they link spoken word with comedy because poets will come and perform for free, and it's really a hot movement right now. But what happens is that you go into an environment that has not been cultivated to appreciate your work, your words or the fact that you are trying to share the art of poetry from your soul. Now, not all nightclubs do this. Not all nightclubs pimps the passion of a person's craft for profit. Not all night clubs have event coordinators and promoters whose primary concern is so much for money and popularity that they are willing to sacrifice the elevation of the ART by exploiting it in an atmosphere that damages its integrity, creditability and pure artistry.

Never Meant to Hurt You
A Rapist's Apology Performed at NPS 09 West Palm Beach Florida

SHELLZ) My first porn flick was real! Live and in color right beside me.

Mike) It wasn't from the television's flashing lights or from windows late at night

AJ/SHELLZ) It was a cinema of torn hymens, sitting in silence beside me!

BIG ANT) PEEK A BOO! I SEE YOU!

Big Ant) Spent most nights imagining what you looked like without that dress on!

A.J) The Scent of lilac, ribbons on pony tails, you were the perfect height,

AJ/ANT) NICE! WE BOTH wanted this RIGHT?

SHELLZ) Monsters were never beneath her bedsprings.

SHELLZ/MIKE) The ones she feared made her mattress their sanctuary

MIKE) Scary like blood stains on motel sheets, cigarette burnt submission…she's

BIG ANT) "Wishing On A Star"

AJ/BIG ANT) Never Meant To Hurt You!

AJ) Didn't know 10 year-olds could stand as still as statues

SHELLZ) Scratched you, snatched you up like toy poodles.

BIG ANT) Your screams frightened me!

AJ/Big Ant) But you were so damn beautiful!

MIKE/SHELLZ) Being frightened by screams is no excuse to keep ripping and tearing, and biting and pushing, deeper… you hurt me…

AJ) Unwelcomed hands should never leave palm prints on soul .

SHELLZ) She shakes with each rock of the bed.

Big Ant) Never meant to hurt you.

A.J.) Just wanted to touch your hair!

Big Ant) Never meant to hurt you.

AJ) Felt so good down there….

SHELLZ/MIKE) Don't know how we got here!

Big Ant) Here is where we once stitched stars to storm clouds

MIKE) Where bits & pieces of boys lay scattered among the shadows of broken men

A.J) Tried to fix it with each tear I shed,

BIG ANT) Ghosts still haunt her bed

SHELLZ) But no tears could ever wash away fingerprints on torn panties.

Never Meant to Hurt You *(Continued)*

MIKE) MY FIRST PORN FLICK WAS REAL YA'LL!

SHELLZ) Teeth marks on young thighs leave scars that last a lifetime

AJ) Never Meant To Hurt You

AJ/MIKE) We Taste Here

Big ANT) WE RAPE.. HERE! **AJ)** Never meant to hurt you.

SHELLZ) SOMEBODY MAKE THEM STOP **Big Ant) NO!**

AJ) NEVER MEANT TO HURT YOU!

AJ/BIG ANT) NEVER MEANT TO HURT YOU!

AJ/MIKE/BIG ANT) NEVER MEANT TO HURT YOU!

(SHELLZ) GIVE HER BACK INNOCENCE.

MIKE) PLEASE! SHE WANTS TO BE FREE!

AJ) I OFFER NO APOLOGY **SHELLZ)** NO COMFORT **(BIG ANT)** FORGIVE US!

AJ) I CAN'T HELP IT! **AJ) I** Never…. **Shellz)** Meant…. **BIG ANT)** To Hurt You.

MIKE) **RUN!**

Because of this, pure poetry open mics are quickly becoming a lost tradition. One that used to provide spaces that truly embraced and nurtured the purity of poetry. In essence...those venues became HOME.

Do you think nightclubs know or care that they are destroying the fabric of a tradition that for years has been the foundation for some of the most prolific voices in literature today? There are countless venues that truly make an effort to provide that space. THAT HOME for new and old voices.

It's time for poets and spoken-word artists to stop allowing themselves to be used as part of a gimmick by night clubs whose main concern is dollar signs and bar tabs and not the elevation of this art. How are we as artists ever going to reach a level of respectability and comparable compensation if we continue to allow ourselves to be exploited this way? What we bring forth with our work is an art that is gaining new life and a resurgence in the literary and entertainment communities.

Its value has never been more evident than in Tyler Perry's new movie, Madea's Family Reunion. The entire film from beginning to end was laced with poetry and spoken word. The poem by the sister at the club, the fusion of Poetry's Matriarch Ms. Maya Angelou and the spoken-word speech by Ms. Cicely Tyson at the reunion. All of this is proof that what we do has value, purpose, and is the reason why we should reap all the benefits of our art.

NOW NOT ALL NIGHT CLUBS DO THIS. I Repeat not all nightclubs and other businesses only see what we do as a way of boosting profits and not the art form. Some actually care enough about the movement to provide a space... JUST FOR POETS! I suggest you seek out THOSE venues and take your poetry BACK!

Be better writers, better self promoters, exercise better judgment in choosing venues in which you speak.

And when you do.. Speak. Speak well and command an audience.

There is a renewed sense of self that is lending to a re-emergence of poetry and spoken word as a voice for the people.

It's up to us to step up and answer the call by doing everything we can to promote our art in places that truly embrace it. How are we ever going to get a Grammy category or a BIG book deal if we allow what we know is a viable voice in the industry, TO BE DEMENANED FOR CLUB GREEN?

Now I am not the most eloquent or well-read brotha or well spoken for that matter. And I too have been a participant in this, but now I know better... and I also know and realize that you guys are my voice as well as God's instruments, and it is all of our collective responsibilities to support those who support THE ART AT ITS PUREST!

It's up to the poets and poetry lovers to support venues that provide that space, that HOME where our art can flourish. It's time to hold these promoter-pimps accountable. Poets, your work has value. If it did not, the venue would not be promoting your craft as entertainment. Recognize and Realize that. OK?

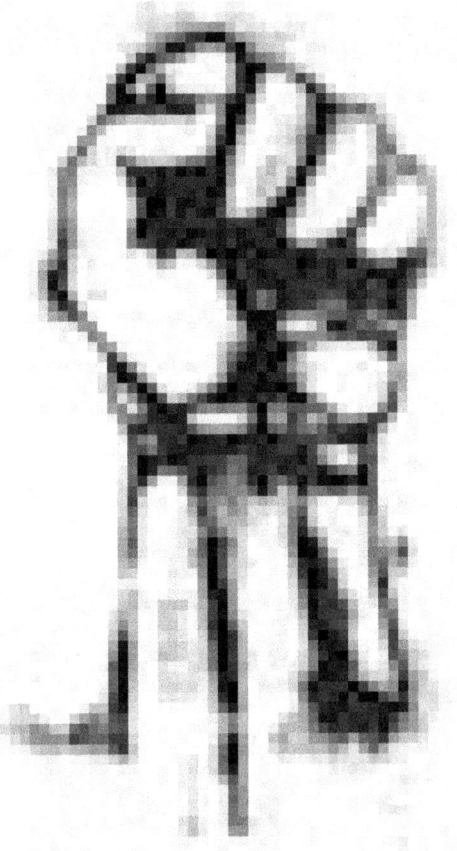

POWER To POETRY

WWW.MIKEGUINN.COM
(817) 412-3964

STOLEN FROM AFRICA
ORIGINAL POEMS FROM THE SOUL OF A REINCARNATED SLAVE
BY MICHAEL GUINN-MSW

Photo Borrowed from Harlem Book Festival

WE WILL NEVER BE SLAVES AGAIN

Heaven's Highway

Love is like making short trips with many pit stops.
Especially if the person you chose to ride with, drives a Yugo.

No matter how careful or how much time and maintenance you invest in this Yugo,
you always end up breaking down on love's highway and in need of expensive
repairs.

Eventually, this driver winds up speeding blindly over jealous hills and careening around
cheating curves, crashing internally.

Love is then a total lost. Reckless maneuvers of the heart no doubt
Who could have known that your passenger side airbags would be filled with hot air and
not affection.

Still you ignored all the road signs and listened to back-seat drivers give shifty
directions. Now... you are lost... and there is no map to aid in your heart's location.

So with a gangster lean, you cry on shoulders of one-way roads, and dead end streets.
All because of un-steered devotion. What a pity.

Slowly, you cruise around love's projects, messing up your wheel alignment with each
speed bump of betrayal. Your house... is surely... not a home.

Finally, you coast into that empty parking lot of broken hearts. Your self-esteem now at
its all time low. Not knowing what's worse living or living without, you begin frantically
flipping sex switches, opening sin roofs, never even bothering to look at the operator's
manual. Spinning your wheels because you have no grip on life, no traction.

Stuck in muddy desperation and helpless you try to steer your Yugo onto the road of love
again.

But you just end up scratching gears of emotions, shifting years in reverse.

So one day you pull in to God's service station and refuel your mind and heart with food
for the soul.

Filling up on biblical twinkies and holy hostess cupcakes quenching that spiritual thirst.
(Can I get an amen?)

As you are about to leave, you notice a sign that says, "Yield Right Of Way" to
"INCOMING ANGELS."

This route of chaos seemingly has turned into Heaven's Highway with all lanes HOV.

You now realize that you were never lost ...just on the wrong damn road.
Please get on the right road!

I

*I
Come to you
Bare
Naked
My emotions all but exposed
But here*

*I am
I
Come to you
Half of a whole
That has no half to hold
But still*

I

Come

To

You

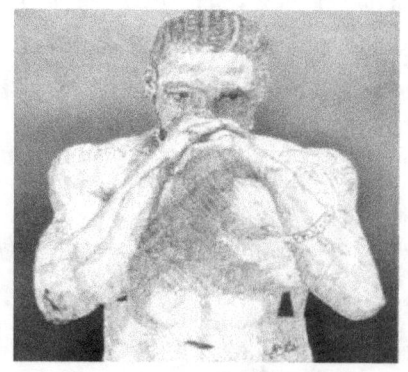

By Litza Boden

Slipping Through Cracks

Great Granny at 43, addicted to crack.
And Grandma, 30, makes her living on her back.
Without hope new mothers learn old tricks.
A daughter's innocence stolen before the age of 6.

Plant their feet on solid ground, now how can they do that?
When generations before them keep slipping through
the cracks.

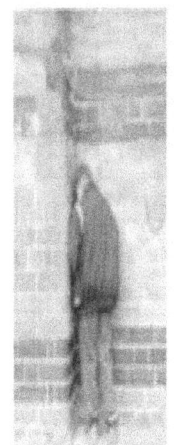

Great grandfather's a magician disappeared at 60.
Grandpa plays the field no responsibilities at 50.
Daddy likes children, touching his favorite game.
Grandpa and daddy are both one in the same.

We tell our children be productive become positive impacts.
But they just cry because through blind eyes,
they keep slipping through the cracks.

Brothers become cousins and Uncle, momma's friend.
Lil" sistah hides her feelings in secret closets of sin.
High School sophomores at 18, chilling having fun
while flippin' burgers 2 counts of murder, twice convicted at 21.

Go to school be successful, now how can they dream that?
When the only examples they have to follow keep slipping through
the cracks?

Comets of despair, asteroids of destruction.
Meteors of hate create black holes of dysfunction.
What can we do, me and you, to turn their lives around?
Break the cycle, and stop generations from cultural meltdown.

The Grim reaper their brother's keeper, death's train is on their tracks.
Growing up is just pure luck for a child slipping through the cracks.

ONE

Somewhere near the end of time.
Tears wash away stains
left upon the fabric
of our souls.

Freedom flows freely.
Dreams and life meet for the first time
and we become one.

We become one you and I.
Humble

As we stumble
In and out life's jungle

But still
we
remain
as
One

Photo by Litza Boden

A Kiss

It's your kiss, I taste.
Your touch I feel each time I hold the hand of another.
And your breath I breathe,
I'll never be free.

You are the Spring of my winter, Sun of my moon,
Your smile is the warmth that melts frozen whispers.
Thaws icy emotions releasing the man inside.

Your love is the strength that burns my heart with a fire
that takes my spirit higher and fills me with desire.

And as I run marathons of tip-toed desperation.
I cry... begging God to let me find you again.
But here I am... still waiting for you.

Stormy Moments

As I listen to the falling rain.
I close my eyes and watch tiny naked Pygmy women dancing
near a waterfall of sound.

This moment creates a stream of free flowing rhythm
that chases the tide of my life.
And I realize that I'm crying inside.

The thunder so loud and frightening.
Reminds me of the stormy times
and how much I miss the sunrise in your eyes.
Still morning denies my escape to the next day.

As I breathe in silence,
I inhale the freedom hope brings.
Exhaling the stormy moments that remain.

Art By Litza Boden

THERE

In a field full of roses and memories,
destiny beckons us near.
Wrapped in a rainbow of harmonies,
I see you there.

Foolish I was to caress thee.
A wild moments weakness we share.
Careless we bow to the fantasy.
But do we dare?

Helpless I reach for your melody.
Caught in the eclipse of your stare.
Still so much more than a mystery,
didn't mean to scare.

Seeking, I search for a way to see
a woman, a diamond so rare.
All we have are whispers of dreams to be
and I miss you there…

I miss you…

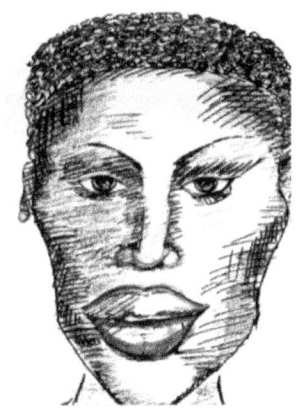

Faith

One believes

that believing becomes our reasoning.

But as life and death succumb to the sounds of night and day,

we pray for freedom to be FREE!

Flight be redeemed in defiance of

Murphy's Law

As tears skate along the edge of lifelines.

Circling eyes devoid of logic and language.

Curse a silence that refuses to sleep.

But as freedom rips free of being,

souls slip from their bondage.

Faith flourishes stronger than now

greater than this moment

fueled by a power

higher than the breath of being free.

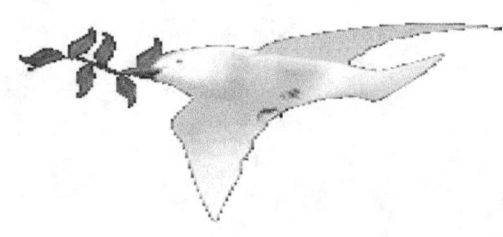

IF I HAD ONE WISH
By Michael Guinn

If I had a million wishes!
I'd wish to ride in Heaven's Rodeo with a lasso of tassels and wrestle golden calves till halves become whole and you and I... become... ONE.

Whenever I'd pray!
I'd ask Jesus please take my pieces and turn my suffering into an oasis of infinitives until my heart cares about more than my own soul...because yours is the only light I ever want to hold.

If I had a hundred lifetimes!
I'd simply wish to walk with your hand in mine galloping into the sunshine of your smile. And as moonlight becomes a ministry of kisses, our hearts would dance to anthems of hoof prints in kingdoms of magic and majesty.

If I had ten genies!
I'd wish to climb down from the mountain inside, just to play double-dutch with the electricity of your smile and watch as the lightening from angels playing hip hopscotch... skip beats across the landscape of our souls and I'd never let go... NOT... unless God Told Me So!
You see I'd love you that much.

IF I HAD ONE WISH *(Continued)*

If I could receive a miracle!
It would be to become your spiritual cowboy, ride twilight's bronco, bareback like stallions of forever's and never let go of morning's magnificent mustang, until mercy curses me at an altar of ancestors celebrating mother nature's anniversary.

But tonight ... all I need is ONE WISH!
*Cause this love be wild and free and we'd be holding on like it's the last time we'd ever ride sunsets. And I'll be clutching the light love left inside with all my might until God tells me ...**"Michael... It's ok son... you can let go now."***

*She's not going **anywhere!** You're in Heaven ...remember? Your rodeo days....are over.... No more rough rides on storm clouds. No more running from your own thunder nor need to wonder, just new love on that old ranch in the sky. And that's where you and I'd never part cause to live without you would be blasphemy...cause without you there's just half of me. You see.. I'm need of spiritual resurrection. But I'd gladly settle to simply live forever in the Heaven of your eyes...**And All I Need... Is... One Wish.***

Michael Guinn is a professional writer who is also one of the world's top performance Poets. To book Michael for your next event call (817) 412-3964 or email jordanmichaelg@yahoo.com and visit Michael at www.mikeguinn.com.
(Workshop and media appearances included) ©2001

RESUME FOR FRIENDSHIP

Dear Beautiful Women Of the World:

Please receive this resume as an official application for friendship. It is my hope that you seriously consider this document as a patient reminder that when the time is right, I'm willing to be more than just your friend. My one and only prayer is that when you are ready for a man who'll be faithful, loyal, and dedicated to making you happy for the rest of your life, that you'll consider a good man for that honor.

In the meantime, I'll be more than content to simply be your FRIEND without benefits! Sincerely with all my heart and soul...

A Good Man Who's Willing To Wait For Love

POSITION: Friend with benefits and/or a chance for romantic advancement.

DATE OF APPLICATION: TODAY! RIGHT NOW! PRONTO, ASAP!

Applicant's Appearance: Height –Forever. **Age:** An ageless dynamo with a dark complexion, medium-brown eyes, bald head, athletic build, huge heart, lots of energy and a devilishly delicious smile Oh and huge feats. ***He winks***

TALENTS: The art of Performance Poetry, conversation, and caring from my heart.

PERSONALITY: Spontaneously affectionate, chivalrously dependable, and playfully seductive.

STRENGTHS

Thoughtful and compassionate. dedicated, committed and loyal.

Spiritually aware and emotionally stable.

Socially conscious, incredibly versatile Financially independent.

Willing to work on any aspect of his life to be the best for the right woman

Energetic and intimately flexible. Romantically sensual and sincere.

Open minded, kind, considerate and remarkably handsome.

Creatively in tune to the feelings of others. Resilient, hardworking and punctual.

Admits when he's wrong and tries hard not to argue.

Cleans up very well and is uncompromising when it comes to the support of friends.

Brings class and intelligence to relationships.

Knows how to treat a lady (A real lady)

Willing and able to love and be loved.

Loves God, loves people, and his self.

Willing to spend the rest of his life making his soul mate happy.

WEAKNESSES

Too thoughtful and compassionate with women incapable of intimate comprehension.

Cares too damn much for those unable and unwilling to appreciate their energy and passion and needs to stop wasting time with those who do not seek

THE HEART OF THE MAN BEHIND THE WORDS!

Wears his heart on his sleeve, at times. Is never jealous. Is always open to suggestions.

Is too supportive, a good listener, and empathetic which gets on the nerves of a woman who is paranoid.

Unselfishly willing to help other people even when he himself needs help.

Knows how to love but chooses wrong woman at the wrong time in her life. (SOS)

Willing to sacrifice, to listen, and to learn how to be the perfect mate.

Heart has been broken which left a slight scar. But has learned that God & time heals all wounds.

Too much of a damn gentleman and too courteous, which is often misconstrued as being too soft or passive or a lack of confidence by today's women's standards.

At least that's the way today's woman views good men because they are so sadly accustomed to men who have dogged them. But we refuse to allow the closed mindedness of the bitter to stop us from seeking our QUEEN!

RESUME FOR LOVE PENDING BECAUSE QUALIFICATIONS FOR THIS JOB CHANGES SPORADICALLY DUE TO SOME WOMEN'S HARDENED HEARTS.

(Disclaimer) Men must learn that some women (not all) can be just as unscrupulous and conniving as any man. Guys, you've got to remember that not every woman **DESERVES** a good man and that some may even be too heart scorned to appreciate one even when God presents him. If you want to be friends and you meet the criteria, please call or email us. Other good men are out there accepting applications RIGHT NOW. Fellas, if you're a great guy and you want to find the love of your life. You have my permission to use this application. Just use it for good not for evil and find the RIGHT WOMAN! SHE'S OUT THERE! Job open till filled. (817) 412-3964 or email jordanmichaelg@yahoo.com, Check out www.mikeguinn.com.

Stars are Writing Poetry

Dark skies become nightshade for the hunted. I cry the milky-way.

The stars are writing poetry again
and I, a moon-child,
must listen to words woven by time.

Big words in bold borealis.
Scream an epiphany in streams as they
race across galaxies of discontent.

Meaningless tear-prints leave trails of stardust and sadness, deep, dark, and damned where there is so much space that even the echoes are afraid to venture…

But still… the stars are writing poetry and I, a moon-child, must listen with my soul.

Boneless

In Rwanda… childhood is as long as the lifespan of a flea.
It is a place where fathers sacrifice mothers to save daughters.
Blood runs thinner than water and we still can't solve the equation.
The numbers just keep adding up… Well, it's time to do the math.

Tell me… how many nights must we lie awake watching ancestors stack souls beneath the shadows of old tomorrows? And how many days must we sit stuck like young roaches in the cotton of forgotten eardrums because there, even ghosts won't go near the graveyards the streets have become in Africa? And I'm wondering, does anybody care?
AM I THE ONLY ONE?

Ya see I've been having bad dreams again… been seeing infected soldiers grab little girls by the shoulder smothering young brothers choking from stolen thunder.
And if you'll just close your eyes… you can't help but see pieces of descendants scattered like bacon bits sprinkled like little rotten croutons in a field of crushed skulls.

JUST CLOSE YOUR EYES!… And feel the blade of a rusty machete spilt the nappy scalp of a little girl, slicing off her right eye, ripping off her chin.
Leaving an empty space where her face might have been as if they were rubbed away with an eraser. And I'm getting just a little fucking curious. DOES ANYBODY CARE?
AM I THE ONLY ONE?

Now I know some of you have never seen teardrops turn to toe tags for toddlers never meant to cry mudslides. And maybe you've never been naked on your knees in knots not knowing whether you were going to live or die. And perhaps you can just sit there in your new shoes and FUBU telling your sons and daughters all the SWEET THINGS AFRICA **Used to be.**

But in the land of your mother's fathers those children are crying in colors. And the best thing BET ever did was to give us all a late night conscious, they found a way for you to pay for peace of mind. Well, it's too late. HEAVEN wants her babies back **BONELESS.**

No skeletons no scars, just **BONELESS**, no disease just **FREE.**

And we owe an eternity times three for the souls of billion bold left dying at the foot of a mountain even MARTIN NEEDED WINGS TO CLIMB and I'm sitting at the top with saints who wished they could trade in their wings for those still holding out their hands, hoping to become angels but HEAVEN is running low on halos so they spend limbo at a foster home near the sun.

Where time becomes speed bumps for Section 8 and sunshine. And I'm putting my wings on layaway. I'll be paying for em with POETRY.

Here take it…it's all I've got. But it'll never be enough to be worthy of the AFRICA still fighting for life inside me. **TAKE IT!**

Cause it's time to do the damn math. Time to divide chills times death divided by us times we. Ya see I'm so damn tired of having bad dreams. And someday I'll stop crying crayon colored anthems long enough to stop wasting my life when they had none.

Someday… I'll be as brave as that 6-year-old triple amputee begging for her life.. I'll try to stand for something. Because we've all got work to do… IF we're ever gonna earn those wings…

On the Inside

Inside we walk toward this light that beckons us to look deeper within our being.

And wonder… is it true what we're seeing?
Or is it our souls fleeing the truth of our reality?

There's a space deep inside where old memories die.
They sway aimlessly toward a pit and sit next to sadness,
this place is called madness.

In that space, our souls become so cold that it
controls our emotions.

And we've all been there…Despair!

But while on this journey to our center, we feel the winter of melancholy as tears freeze becoming hell flakes that block our path with no expectations of what is or will be when we finally reach our destiny.

And even though we all gather at the same place on the inside.
On the outside, we smile and pretend.
To me "that" is the greatest sin.

If I'd Known

Of false hopes and erotic wishes
of vultures in their respite.
Some poets speak prose tendering painful reprise.

But my pen simply refuses to sketch the outline of your lies.

Because this is not you. It's just the blue goo oozing inside your thighs.

And if I'd known that the heart breaks forever,
slowly dismantling itself into unrecognizable plots of
misery.

If only I'd known that love leaks its sapphotic sap,
with vulgar invisibility, weaving sin into the
bedrooms of intimate strangers.

And If I'd known that loneliness could stifle joy,
loosen joints and force tongue against cheek
or that despair would confine me,
winding itself around my heart in beautiful unsettling.

And that you, with your sassy Episcopalian insolence,
your twisted sappho-sadistic expressions
and knowledge of bittersweet
bisexual delights would hurt me so.

Still, I would have loved you.
But from a distance,
I would have left your ass whole and wholly
for the delicious defecation of those
who wanted more and cared less.

If only I'd known...

After Work Amnesia

I see you on a daily basis
with eyes closed, I still see your faces.
At home, at work and other places,
so many cultures, so many races.

While working, talking, we forget about color.
That line that separates us from one another.
Why can't we just act like sister and brother?
No anger to hide, No hate to smother.

No sense us risking unnecessary heat,
so we all continue to be discreet.
Toleration is then the only feat,
we both perpetuate and then repeat.

We make feeble attempts to avoid the traps
of hate, indifference, anti social mishaps.
Sooner or later we will perhaps,
choose to ignore this memory lapse.

I Still Follow
A Heaven Triloet

With passion I still follow,

dreams I may not reach.

On a path of new tomorrows,

with passion I still follow.

Hope is what I borrow,

from ancestor's dying speech.

With passion I still follow,

dreams I may not reach.

DON'T JUST BE ALL YOU CAN, BE MORE!

THE LIST
Things You Should and Should Never Do

Never call a woman the "B" Word
Never call your homies the "N" Word
Always listen with an open mind
Have good manners
Have good hygiene
Have some class and style
Try not to sag cause it looks sloppy
Be willing to try new things
Be willing to share
Have good taste in music (ALL MUSIC)
Dance don't bump-n-grind
Use lotion
Clip your finger and toenails
Be aware of your breath
Expect a woman to take care of herself too

If you do all these things,
Not only will you be showing respect for the woman. But you'll be showing respect for yourselves.
MEN, IT'S TIME TO BE MEN!

Hear Me...Free Me

Written Especially For Lauren Calhoun

While listening with my mind
I heard the vicious sound of screaming words over and over again
And I begged to be free

If I could have spoken
I would've told you that I loved you

But how could words break free of words that confined worlds
How could pride blossom under a sun
That you refused to let me feel or see

But someday... I will
Someday I'll be free

What a hefty price I've paid to stay here
What a cruel, cruel game this has been

Twisting in tight spaces to get a better seat
Gasping through keyholes for something to eat

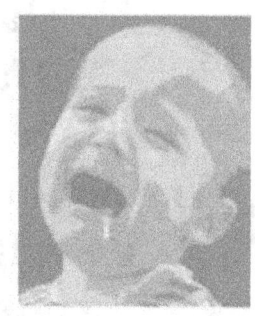

I tried to speak to you through my silence
I tried to tell you that I loved you still
And I always will

But "Daddy"
If you'd only listened close enough
You would have felt the tremble of my heart pounding for your smile
"Momma"
If you'd only listened long enough
You would have heard the poetry pouring from my eyes

And if you both are listening with your hearts RIGHT NOW!!
You just might hear me crying out to you

Because I'm crying in colors
Forming rainbows in the sky
Where tears become raindrops and eyes never lie

And the love born inside me will never, ever die

For as long as I breathe...
The need to be will live forever inside of me
All I ask is that you
Hear me
See me
Set
Me
Free

Malcolm Jamal Warner and Mike Guinn at the Black Academy of Arts and Letters 9/27/09

Black Words

Black Words scribbled on brown days
become invisible when you've got da blues.

The sun, always a distant foe, shines a pale shade of day like spoiled
lemons leaving gray streaks that weave nightshade for the blind who crave the
taste of something other than lemonade.

Sneaky shadows creep like moth-infested wind chimes... and time
becomes enslaved by reasons without rhyme. But right now life becomes a fine
line in a place where wine is the only truth they find. If only they knew that this
is what makes them blind.

Dark moons, silver spoons speak with black eyes that spit
ill-conceived warnings, but how can the yawning hide from
moments where incidental rainbows become echoes in search of a freedom
they'll never know?

Now words churn, black burns, I yearn for just a corner of shade where
letters no longer search for meaning. Where rivers of free-flowing destiny float
in patches, creating spaces where peace teaches the speechless that in order to get
to this level you have to reach.

You have to reach out for the sound music makes as it dangles its melody of
green leaves upon branches of poet trees. You have to reach out to where words
no longer bear the burden of soul scars or silent disregards... for why we are
there. You have to reach out beyond the shadows and blend into lighter shades
of day somewhere close to roads, pain has already paved.

You have to preach with speech then practice what you preach until you teach
others to reach for spiritual release. Because only then will black words scribbled
on brown days find a place called...Peace.

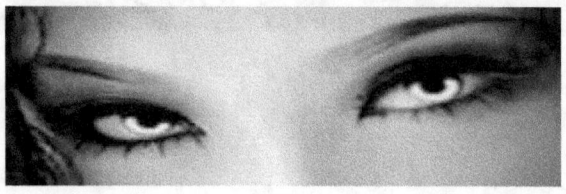

Butterfly Kisses

Your mother... earth, your father... time.
Brother winds, sister rains inside my mind.
My frown your moon...my smile your sun.
Together we'll grow...together as One.

Seeds planted, fertilized with love.
Await blessings from God above.
Hope springs eternal, as roots sprout.
My child, my joy growing up, going out.

That twinkle in my eye is the guiding star.
Tells you where I've been and where you are.
My breath becomes the gentle breeze,
that cools the aches of fragile leaves.

My love goes on forever and a day,
cause little blossoms would wither away.
Petals would dry on brittle stems.
Baby, I'm the tree, you're the limb.

If ever I needed a single wish,
I'd wish for a butterfly's gentle kiss.
Snatch time by the hand of another day.
And keep you safe, from harm's way.

In twinkling eyes, hope dances,
tears water seeds of chances.
Seasons change, tilled by time.
Spirits grow in fertile minds.

At that glorious moment your flowers bloom.
I'll be watching by the light of a bright full moon.
Thanking God for granting wishes.
As you receive your Butterfly kisses.

They Speak Through Me

It's time for me to face my demons…because I…keep seeing her, a mentally challenged teen named Francine, lying on the floor at the back door of a short yellow bus, giving birth to a 3 pound 6 ounce bouncing baby disability. She…was too young to be a mother when we discovered her child born deformed, blind with no arms, no hope, just moments from a pine box in the sun.

Now, it's up to me to fix it. Twist it…and make it all fit.
But… No-one seems to care about an infant, not meant to be sent… broken and bent.
Who'll find a home for the hopeless… dying from cultural fibrosis.
Whose going to do that?…ME.   You see…this is MY JOB!

Seems just like yesterday, I was assigned to collect the bits and pieces of skin still stuck to the pull-ups of a 2-year-old black boy in Fort Worth Texas.

His mother's boyfriend …had tied a shoe string around his penis to keep him from wetting the bed. Then… put a gun to his head and said. "Pee again little…NIGGAH… PEE AGAIN!" And oh how he must have suffered from being bound that way, found face down drowned in his own muddy tears. And as I closed his eyes for the last time. I couldn't stop shaking. But I… had to… SUCK IT UP…and do… THE DAMN JOB!

And every time I've stepped to the mic… I've wondered why …I …bring this darkness. As I listen to other poets, I wish that I could do what they do.

Hell, I want to write funny poems… too!…but I can't. I have a job to do…to be their voice. Because through me… they speak. The ghosts of the weak, restless spirits wandering like secondhand smoke, floating in the abyss of this emptiness.

Through me …THEY SPEAK… the cruelties of being trapped in places where shadows tap dance on hopes, plucking the souls of innocent children… like black roses

Left…..dangling like lil' Heaven puppets.   And now I know…that nightmares… are just dreams too afraid to tell the truth.

BUT…I'VE GOT A JOB TO DO… creating miracles on pages, with the ink of a pen BLEEDING from within. Because THIS … is how… poets …cry. It's how…. I cry.

So tonight… is for all those empty wheelchairs and 20 inch coffins.
Tonight is for all those lonely faces on milk cartons and the terrible memories
I see still sittin' inside your eyes. And YOU… ain't gotta say nothing,
I know that stare too well.

So …there'll be no funny poems from me tonight… because spoken word has a purpose, a reason… and a voice. And I don't want this to sound like itty bitty criticisms but I had to get this pain outta my system because it was clogging up my wisdom.

And soon… …maybe we'll all be more than just poetic paraplegics crippled from all the VERY BAD things we've seen. And someday maybe someone will save the child STILL dying inside. But til then….I'll KEEP ON WRITING FOR THEM. BECAUSE THOSE CHILDREN SPEAK!! …THROUGH ME!

Violation

Tonight, she fondles herself with imagination as she lies there next to me.
I am awake in her slumber, stepping ever so softly so as not to stir
the demons that taunt her daydreams as she screams out his name!!!
And as I walk the path of past men and their foreign tongues,
I wonder will she ever see me standing there?

For now, she sleeps only to be awaken to the cries of children living
in between the cracks of walls that speak the old testament of project
buildings, while those, denied tomorrow, haunt time in yesterday's
laughter leaving her to mumble old Negro spirituals.

And as she stumbles in mid-sleep,
tossing and turning in memories of nothing,
she searches the shadows of a distant reality to find a precious virginity
taken at the height of midnight by a drunken relative.
But this type of violation is done on a daily basis
far from teenage fantasies and Cinderella fairytales,
far from little red riding hoods as its written
by those who lack proper menstrual penmanship.

Lust is just a four-letter key used to unlock.
Forbidden pleasures of hidden treasures with inches of sick wisdom.
But this is how some men measure their manhood.
"FORGIVE THEM FATHER, for they know not what they've done."

And even though she tries to separate herself from reality
she still chooses sex over romantic notions
and her sun simply refuses to shine.

For now she'll continue to fondle herself with imagination.

Perhaps I'll try to move the moon again tonight.
But I know she will never see me in any other light.

A New Foundation

Now first we will begin by salvaging lessons from our past.
And then lay the "black-prints" for our children's future that last.
Now for tools, we'll use leadership bricks.
Iron will as glue and love to ensure that it sticks.

Black History is the model from which we will mold
because on this project, we can't afford to fold.
Then from coals of injustice that still smolder.

We'll begin the search for more, strong, black soldiers.
To instill in our children, a sense of 'strength and black pride.
This assures a good framework for their future un-denied.
Yall… we have to be the Queens and Kings of our community
because our children's future depends on us seizing that opportunity.

To teach the resilience of a people, history chose to trample.
We become Christian role models, and become God's example.
With everyone working together, no matter how little
we can avoid building a foundation that in the past has been brittle.

Keeper of My Sun

Yesterday
I was running barefoot on white sands
My heart was light
My spirit soared
And I was FREE

But as the day succumbed to night
And the moon beat down my sun
I heard foreign whispers
The sound of suspicious metal
And my brother laughing wildly in the wind

From hostile shadows sprang ivory ghost
Grabbing my sistah screaming
Beating my father bleeding
Raping my mother crying
Killing the Africa in me

And all I could do was run
I ran fast as cheetah but could not elude
the giant spider suspended in now enemy trees

While struggling...I was strangled, while fighting... I fought
As the cold embrace of wet chains gripped
my soul, binding my pride with iron rope
And I was no longer "FREE"

Kicking, biting spirit whipped, beaten bloody salty tears stain lips
And all I could do was scream
WHY MOTHER AFRICA WHY!!

But through swollen eyes I saw my brother
laughing with the devil, drinking purple water and I knew
I would never be free again because he held the key to my freedom and
was the keeper of my sun.

Gone in an Instant

My first response was to quickly turn away.
Another child silenced and now sadly...lay
beaten by the hands, that fed and bathed.
Relentless and brutal, his emotions scathed.

Broken bones, crushed toes, fingers bent in two.
Torn clothes, bloody nose, skin shades of blue.
Soaked in a puddle of blood, urine, and stool.
Beaten beyond recognition on his way to school.

Removed from his nails, pieces of daddy's gritty skin.
No "God" should tolerate this malicious act of sin.
How could this happen to child so defenseless?
To murder a child is so cold and senseless.

Neglected and abandoned by a drunken teenage mother.
At age ten his only sin was protecting his little brother.
A fight for his life was waged that day.
Gone in an instant, now daddy has to pay.

No jury will deny this murderous intent.
Of a felon whose crime, no one could prevent.
Justice was swift, a guilty verdict was given.
Death is the penalty to the killer of children.

Dandelions in the Wind

The day was as cloudy as my heart.
    Rain mixed with teardrops, formed life-scrapes within the frowns on my face.
        And now...I'm cry in colors again.

        How can something so cruel be so beautiful?
          How can the sunshine find my sky?
            Warm my heart?
              Soothe my soul?
                When I have
                      no one to hold.

      How can I take another breath?
    Breathe this air?
  Ever inhale again....without her?
Because her love was the air I breathed.

    Night has become a prison of loneliness.
  The telephone tortures me because it refuses to ring.
It hurts worse then being born... Oh how I wish I were born a flower.

Because if I were a flower, then maybe I would not feel so ugly and thrown away.
If I were a flower maybe she would have loved me for my beauty, even if for a moment.

Because even that moment would have been longer than the short span of time I spent in her eyes.

Because in her eyes my love had the lifespan of a weed in a garden of forget-me-nots.

If only she knew that everyday my love would have been as fresh as any rose, as bright as any lily, sweeter than a Sun-flower in June.

But right now... way deep down inside my mind, my thoughts race out of control with nowhere to go.

Those thoughts no matter how crazy always seem to find their way back to the agony of her absence.
    I miss her
        I love her
            But still... here I am all alone...and my heart is left to
                    chase dandelions in the wind.

Death of Dreams

Mama's Poem

She moaned for a moment, silently kicking against the weight of an innocent tree,
before slowly succumbing to the beckoning of the Lord's light.

My mama died today...

Fragile like a small bird, yet to become complete
left dangling in the wind like a forgotten piece of meat.

That rope... wrapped tightly around her until the strangling sounds became a soft
gurgle, and then ....no more. And, even though no one else could see or hear or feel it, I saw
death envelop her moments before she drew her last breath.
It reached out, from that dark place, where souls go, climbed limb by limb till its
obedient assassin of rope enmeshed itself around her neck, and squeezed and squeezed and
squeezed.

The part of her that once sang for joy, despite the woes of bondage
now looked hideously stretched to fit the magnitude of hatred running rampant
through the land.

The eyes that once danced with life, as she'd whisper stories to us in the night
about places we may never see or things we would never do, except on the wings of her
dreams. Now bulged out like black pearls, staring, yet never again to see.

My mama died today...

And in that same instant, gone were the meaning and
reasons that had given substance to the ill-logic of being born in a place and time in which
being hated and hunted was a way of life.

Gone were the arms that held me, when no one was looking, the lips that brushed my forehead
with kisses when I was afraid, and the soft voice that
comforted me when the night riders became the ghosts in my dreams and the reality of my
days.

My mama died today...

Leaving me gasping for knowledge,
longing for the wisdom I would need to survive.
And although weak and afraid, I knew that no matter what,
I could not crumble beneath the weight of what was to come,
No matter what! I could not afford to lose my way, existing in this skin, in this time... so far
away from home.

Because my mama died today...
And as pain erupted like ten thousand volcanoes beneath my skin
I knew in that moment .....That I ....would never climb trees again.

Written By Michael Guinn and Lisa Lacy-Tarer McGriff

Chocolate Kisses

*Slipping...Sliding in chocolate hazes
Dipping...diving in sugar dazes
My donut glazed... my tip ablaze
How I long for sips of your milky ways*

*I only needed reeses reasons
To taste the taste of chocolate seasons
To sniff wild cherry its smell so pleasin'
To taste the Hershey touch of teasin'*

*Come pour yourself a cup of me
Liquid emotion stirred with ecstasy.
Brittle skittles little bites and nibbles
of sinful gems and M and Ms.*

*Mr. Goodbar in mounds of Almond joy.
Juicy fruits, Babe Ruth's and Chips a Hoy
Crunching ...Munching with all I've got.
With Krispy Kremes and Red Hots.*

Desperately clinging to coco dreams

Flooded moments of Toffee screams
*Mingled bodies... melted wishes.
Chocolate is the taste of kisses.*

When a Man Cries

When a man cries...
It is a process that begins from deep within his soul
and takes hold of all he was and will be.

His tears form a kaleidoscope in the dark
as he embarks on a journey toward the light.

But like roots being torn from the earth
his heartache rips at the night
as he fights to hold back the flood of emotion,

But...he can't hold back the emotions.
Because he's not that strong.

So the bow breaks and he begins to shake.

His eyes, still, quickly fill with rivers until
he no longer sees....the need....to be.

But if you venture close enough,
You just might see the little boy inside his eyes.

And if you sit long enough
you just might feel the rhythm of shadows
dancing near his tears.

And if you happen to open your mind to this moment
you just might hear him moaning in shades of blue.

RECOGNIZE

HEY! HEY! Christian Woman... Over here!
You know I get so sick and tired of hearing all these complaints about how there aren't any good Christian men out there. Well, that's not true. You see I tried to recognize you a long time ago but you refused to recognize me. Remember?

I'm the man who watched you walk into tomorrow placing time and distance between us with sorrow. I'm the man who was willing to be your man. Hey, I'm over here. Right here where I've always been just begging for a chance to get to know you better. But I guess my eyes couldn't shout loud enough to get your attention. Remember Me?

I used to drive that Volvo and had a runny nose but I suppose too much of me was revealing and unappealing because you threw your nose up in the air and rolled your eyes at the ceiling. Remember?

I'm the one who opened that door at the store, left that little note on your windshield where I'd scribbled a poem on a grocery receipt just because I was so inspired by your smile. And if you'd just smiled at me once in a while. You'd be smiling instead of frowning right now.

But I was a forgettable part of your past, because I didn't have the flash or the cash, but what you didn't recognize was that I would have worked my butt off for you. Woman a good man doesn't always stand 6'4 ...and big feet don't always mean more. And it doesn't have to have hair on his head, instead he could just look like me, maybe one day you'll see. But while you were losing sleep over that brother you figure was the bomb. I was working, perfecting this poetry, flowing, growing, showing that there was much more to me than the eye could see.

And if you'd just taken the time to notice, if you'd just taken the time for prayer, I would have been right there where God told me to be and you wouldn't be all alone. But now all you got is drama because that brother you figure was the bomb was just a boy and your body was his toy. You let him play with your emotions and he stole your joy. So now you sit there upset, refusing to reflect on how you disrespected yourself. That's why that little man-boy left. Left you with KOOL-AIDS. No sugar. A Baby with Boogers. No money for diapers and one windshield wiper on that same raggedy old car, that I left a thousand receipts under.

And you know what? It don't even run anymore. But he does.

And no need to wonder where he goes, just ask your girlfriends, they know.

So next time someone is screaming across the room with their eyes, open your heart and listen to love. HEY DO YOU SEE ME NOW?

FIGHT
An Original Poem for Victims of Domestic Violence

You have to be one of the bravest women God ever made.
Your courage can only be described as motivational.
Your walk with favor nothing short of inspirational.
This battle! Your battle!!
Is one of incredible strength and resilience?
Your brilliance is like a million points of light bursting with life.

And we could never know the
struggle of just breathing.
And we could never how you
kept on praying and believing.
But you did!
Why because you knew how to fight.
Armed with faith and that
stuff black women are born with.
YOU FIGHT!

To be free of pain and misery
YOU FIGHT!

Because you will not be denied. This will not keep you down...

SO YOU PRAY, YOU BELIEVE, YOU FIGHT!
It's what Strong Christian women do.
And Nothing. Not even assault or battery
could ever replace the most precious blessing
God ever gave! The Gift of Resilience!
So be strong my sister, keep your
head up, grit those spiritual teeth...
AND FIGHT!

Benefit of the Doubt

I've noticed you following closely while I shop
As I browse I feel your eyes stare then stop
Your subtle suspicion by itself is admission
That it's my color and not my actions
that prompt inquisition

What is it about me that fits your profile?
Could it be that you see my skin and not my style
This is obviously a case of false disparity
You've seem to make a habit of mistaken similarity
Why have you miss-took me for this common thief
Nervously phone security based on personal belief

You refuse to believe I have the ability to pay
In your mind, you see me as part of society's decay
Abject humiliation precede this moral attack
Heavily fueled by the reality that I happen to be black

You'd think sober judgment would
thwart this embarrassment
This intentional breach of privacy
borders on harassment

Why deny me the courtesy
that for years I've done without?
So for once please grant me
the Benefit of the Doubt

In Your Eyes

Each night, I am awakened by soft whispers calling me, calling me, as winter winds swirl inside my mind, creating heart-shaped clouds
guided by love's gentle breeze.

I am simply driven insane by your presence,
cause I've been digging' you for awhile now.
Don't you know that it takes everything I have to contain my hunger
because my admiration is not just infatuation,
but a fixation on the woman inside.

Within your eyes, I see blue flames of fires
lit with mental match sticks,
fueled by passion's kindling
as it burns to new heights,

I want to be the man that lights your eternal fire.

EVERYDAY
The Erotic Version - By Michael Guinn

If I could capture a rainbow, I'd wrap you in my favorite colors and paint you perfect.

Because every day, all I do is look for ways to do and say more than I did the day before ...
to tell you how much I love you!
And right now all I want to do... all I ever want to do...

If I could capture a rainbow.
I'd wrap you in my favorite colors and paint you perfect. Because every day, all I do is think of ways to do and say more than I did the day before. To tell you just how much I miss you. And right now. All I want to do.
All I ever want to do is to taste you Tuesdays, wake you Wednesdays.
Quench your Thursdays till Friday
then sit Saturdays sipping your
Sundays 'til Monday.
You see I want to love you daily.

I want you to get sprung in the Spring sizzle in the Summer
Feast on me falling, calling as you and I anticipate the Autumn, and get buck wild below the waist in Winter.

Because my love... is all the seasoning you'll need.

I want you to go crazy as I slide off your Januarys
Pull down your Februarys, March right up in between your Aprils as your May becomes June and your July... lays naked in the August of my September until you remember that October... was when my naughty November eased inside your delicious December.
Listen... All I'm trying to say is
I want to love you
EVERYDAY!

The Color of Freedom

*Sitting all alone
I've become afraid of the future
Uncertainty brings*

*There's a rhythm beating
deep down inside
But there's no song there*

*Often I cry because
It seems as though I was born at the wrong time
In the wrong place
The wrong color
A disgrace for being me*

*You can see this on my face
Day and night, night and day
Oozing from my pores
Inside the lion snores*

*I'm terrified of the enemy freedom has become
I am lost in this hunger for understanding
My heart is dry and thirsty for unspoken libation*

*If I could just get back home…
I know it would not be so hard for me to be me
Because being black would mean more
TO ME BLACK IS THE COLOR OF FREEDOM*

Hold On

They kept tightening nooses.
Tied knots in excuses.
Strangled hope with hate's rope
and rendered pride useless.

They confused revolution with lies, illusions
born free, you and me if they let us be.
But with nowhere to hide if we decided to run
our bodies were enslaved and our freedom... gone.

Locked inside plantation prisons.
Where closed minds bred indecision.
So you and I just cry, screaming Why?
Without faith in each other, we lose, we die.

Shackles heavy, the burden great.
From chains rusty with the weight of hate.
Break these bonds "Lord," it's not too late.
To let hearts explore and spirits escape.

Sir we're begging, pleading, leave us be.
Don't ignore our plea and not set us free .
Pride rottens, pickin' cotton from dusk to dawn.
So release us NOW!! Let freedom live on.

NEW YORK PUBLIC LIBRARY,
SCHOMBURG COLLECTION

Shy Compliments

Silently she sits quietly surveying the room.
Is she married or single?? I can only assume.
From first glance I've noticed her beautiful eyes
luscious lips, curvaceous hips
are just a part of her disguise.

Her smile, hypnotic makes for an exotic potion
as I sit I have to admit that she is, poetry in motion.
Mysterious lady, so nice, so sweet
the smoothest woman,
going or coming any man could meet.

Her presence is that of dreamy perfection.
Her image incites erotic obsession.
Perhaps I'll find a way to convey this sentiment
and tell her, she's beautiful ...my highest
compliment.

Guide to Becoming Real Men

This guide has been created to help guide on their path young men in personal growth and development.

It will address respect for self and others, manners, hygiene, proper dress, and managing emotions.

It will also address the importance of being on time, education, communication, consequences, being responsible, and social awareness.

Please read every damn page of this guide.
Don't skip around or disregard its impact on your manhood.

Because if you do. You may regret it for the rest of your life.

And If I Am Correct. This guide will present you with a foundation that could not only save your life but the lives of your children.

So if you truly want to make a change that leads to you becoming a better human being.
Then please keep reading….

And remember… fellas….

Teachers' mentor-Men model– and our women monitor!

THINGS WOMEN DO THAT GET ON MEN'S NERVES

1. WOMEN LACK UNDERSTANDING OF MAN'S NEEDS.
2. WOMEN WITH BAD BOY BAGGAGE.
3. WOMEN WHO ARE JUST FLAT OUT CRAZY.
4. WOMEN WITH BAD HYGIENE.
5. WOMEN WHO ARE IMMATURE.
6. WOMEN WHO ARE STUCK ON THEMSELVES.
7. WOMEN WHO USE MEN.
8. WOMEN WITH BAD BREATH.
9. WOMEN WITH JACKED UP FEET.
10. WOMEN WHO ARE MELODRAMATIC.
11. WOMEN WHO DON'T KNOW WHAT THEY WANT.
12. WOMEN WHO DON'T CARE ABOUT THEIR HEALTH.
13. WOMEN WHO SPREAD THEIR LEGS TOO EASILY.
14. WOMEN WHO ARE TRIFLING– GOSSIPING –MESSY.
15. WOMEN WHO DON'T RECOGNIZE WHAT TRUE LOVE IS!

THINGS MEN DO THAT GET ON WOMEN'S NERVES

1. MEN WHO ARE DOGS.
2. MEN WHO USE WOMEN.
3. MEN WITH BAD HYGIENE.
4. MEN WITH BAD MANNERS.
5. MEN WHO CAN'T DANCE.
6. MEN WHO CHEAT-LIE-STEAL.
7. MEN WHO ARE STALKERS.
8. MEN WHO WON'T TAKE NO FOR AN ANSWER.
9. MEN WITH ASHY SKIN.
10. MEN WHO ARE BROKE.
11. MEN WITH NO EDUCATION.
12. MEN WHO TRY TO HAVE SEX WITH NO PROTECTION.
13. MEN WHO SMELL.
14. MEN WHO SMACK OR CHEW WITH THEIR MOUTH OPEN.
15. MEN WHO SAG.
16. MEN WITH NOT STYLE—NO CLASS—NO TASTE.
17. MEN WHO DON'T TREAT A WOMAN LIKE A LADY.
18. UGLY MEN-FAT MEN-SLOW MEN-HO MEN.
19. MEN WHO HAVE NO SENSE OF CULTURE.
20. MEN WHO SPREAD DISEASES.
21. MEN WHO THINK LOVE# IS SEX!

You Should Have

I wished I'd known this before
The signs were there,
but I did not care
You should've told me I meant more

I'm suppose to recognize disguise
Your feelings weren't real
If only I'd known not to feel
I probably could've if I'd opened my eyes

If it were me I would have told you
If it were me I would have shown you
Unconditional love sent from above
If it were me I would have loved you

I wish I'd known it was a matter of time
That your heart wasn't in it,
and that your love had its limits
You should've told me you'd never be mine

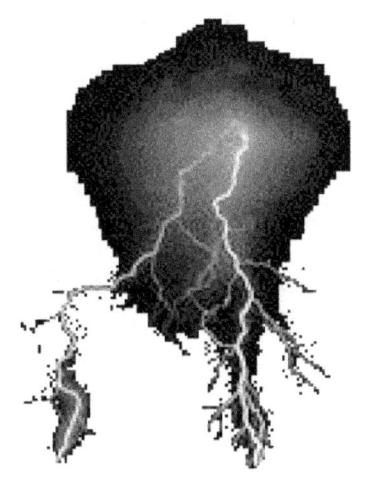

That Rope

Running, hiding from acquisition
hunted, hounded into submission.
Over heard them say "string em up!"
My eyes wide open, my mouth... shut

Lord set me free me from my demise.
Help me fight the fires of burning lies.
But I'm tied in knots, hands and feet
strung up high in a old oak tree.

Its grip -- firm! Its hold, tight!
So cold the blood on that rope that night.
A bowie knife quickly slices an ear
a waiting child's souvenir.

Eyes red with innocent blood
feet heavy with hatred's mud.
Loose bowel vowels, a garbled plea
of cut this rope and set me free.

Jerking, kicking, wondering how
begging pleading, release me now.
Kerosene smell chokes my breath.
Clothes soaked with the scent of death.

That Rope *(Continued)*

A prisoner of my own brown skin
My freedom, gone with the wind
Gasping for justice in empty despair
Hung for nothing in the midnight air

My dying wish, my only hope
Is the Angel coming to cut that rope
In my eyes tears of a beaten warrior
Soul conquered by pride's destroyer

So sad this child, barely eleven
Had to go through hell to get to heaven
That rope I feel, that rope I know
Take me now! let my spirit go

Oh lord please let me in
Being black was my only sin
Rope burned freedom left scars of hate
Written in lashes 2 years 2 late

As fiery crosses burn dismay
I'm Unable to speak, unable to say
Watch out! Sistah, look out brotha!
That rope, that rope awaits anotha!

In My Son's Eyes
(Home) (Inspired By a Cat Stevens Song)

There's a brotha at the club...sitting way back in the shadows sipping on bitter memories. He has a story but its glory has been lost in the cost he paid to get in where he fit in.

2 sons, no wives, empty guns, dull knives and lives wasted, so in the shadows he sits...too afraid to face it.

I was that brotha...and I was so restless that I traveled west in search of the rest of me and left the best of me back there...... in my son's eyes

Every day I think of him.
At lunch I wonder what he's eating
At night I wonder what he's dreaming.
And sometimes I feel his little hands search for mine, his eyes watching the clock waiting for me to drive up... and it's too bad that's how he learned to tell time. And I'm so sorry.

So from this moment on, I promise... that he... will not have to grow up wondering where I am.

He will not have to search for me in his short term memory because I'll be right there.... Where I'm suppose to be. By his side....in his eyes...

That's why I'm going home...today...because I miss him....
I miss him like a poet without an audience...
I miss him like sight from a thousand blind eyes...I miss him.... I miss him I miss him...

And I'm going home...to play catch up... and watch him grow up... not by luck but by practice as I practice becoming a better father...

We gon' read till our mind bleeds, play all day, hug till our arms blister and I become the best at being more than just mister. Till I'm daddy... again. And I promise no more cats in cradles or silver spoons
No more little boy blue, I'm the man your moon
And I'll be going home ...just to see you grin
And we'll stay together then... son...
You know we'll have a good time ... then...

Love ya son...

The Taste of Touch

Here...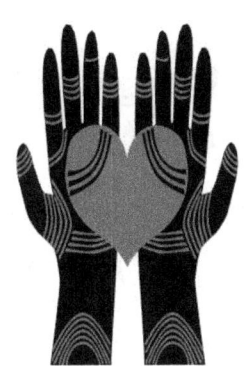

So soft the taste of skin smooth,
silky slippery, as lips slide effortlessly amid
currents of liquid emotion.

Rapidly, romance ripples across quivering limbs
drawn closer with each gentle wave of kisses.

Burrowing hands find you trembling there.

Where a trespass of soft caresses
unfolds, take hold, then separates with passion
unbridled.

We meld into one as emotion heightens and
embrace tightens, subduing perfection with
mental erections creating sensations
indescribable.

I'm in. Cascading slowly, through sensitive folds
of ebony. As chocolate peaks atop mounds of brown stir
constant urges to touch... to taste
that taste of touch.

I Thought of You Today
For J.

For the second consecutive night, I've awakened at 2 a.m.
Got in my car, driven to San Fran, felt the sand and watched the sunrise inside my eyes. You see... I thought of you today...

As I walked that lonely beach, each step left footprints
filled with teardrops that became images of you.
I watched you wink at me, your smile, your laughter and I found myself running barefoot, chasing sea gulls... just to keep up with
the moving picture that your memory had become.

You were a silent cinema stretched out across the shoreline of my mind rewinding the good times we once shared. Your whispers echoed like seashells, your eyes shone like moonlight, your breath moved like trade winds.
I felt your presence and smiled, because for a brief moment... I had you again.

You see... I thought of you today...

And as dawn approached, your face quickly faded into time bubbles bursting from the prick of reality. And no matter what I did, it was simply not enough to sustain the love I'd come to adore and I missed you that much more.

And as your essence disappeared in the distance…
I fell to my knees and tried to recapture the magic of loving the you, you used to be… the you that used to see…me… as the love of your life.

I tried to grab your image from the sand but your face turned away and left me cold. And I wondered how could my arms be so empty for what my heart still holds.

My body collapsed and my face dug deep down in regrettable retreat as my eyes closed and I cried my heart out for the millionth time.

The salt from my tears mixed with the sea and heartache's waves washed over me like God's cold blanket… and I thought… this must be where tears go.

Because I've cried an ocean since you've left… I mean …for me…
it will always be this way… because you see…
I thought of you today… missed you last night and needed you tomorrow.
But I suppose God still has some work to do… because no matter how hard I try or how much I pray…I just can't stop loving you.
So … I just wanted you to know…that I thought of you today…I always do.
And where ever you are or will be…I hope that you…
thought of me… too.

Heart of a Slave

Imagine being hunted, caught, sold then bought…
Your dignity nothing more than an after thought.
Your spirit chained, your soul in knots.
Your history lynched, your future… shot.
And there's a sign over head saying **"Nig-grahs For Sale"**
Imagine this as the beginning of…a living hell.
"STRONG BLACK BUCKS NEEDED AND NIG-GRAH WENCHES FOR
BREEDIN" Imagine your children growing up with only this to believe in.
See yourself standing in shackles, auctioned off like cattle
poked and prodded till your soul rattles.
Then cultivated like black roses, no one to follow not even Moses.
Spreading ya cheeks, showing ya teeth, and other degrading poses

And all day long in dem fields….Corn mush for your meal.
Only then will you know why we'd lie, fight, and cheat to be free.
ONLY THEN WILL YOU KNOW… Only then …
And when you see massa' fat from profits …you'll wonder why God didn't stop
it and then you'll look up scream...   Is we free yet suh? Is we free? **NO**… ain't
freedom for negroes.
Just bare foot winters, hot summers and splinters.
No honeymoons... just shacks, bred like coons out back.
And massa's become matchmakers, peeping toms, and rapist
because they figga, hand on trigga, they can raise corn, cotton, and niggas.

And you… BET …not…. get old cause yo ass **will** get sold.
And running way only meant you'd get killt fa sho.
Ya see no matta what they did all we could do was **DREAM** …
Just dream on bended knee about the day we'd **be free**!

You see slavery was the first fraternity and sorority for this minority.

But somewhere between the plantation of our past, next to the cotton field of our future, there's an old abolitionist on her knees praying for betta tomorrows. But all she's seen …are broken broom sticks and tooth picks in the mouth of a massa up to his old tricks. Trading' father's brothers, sisters and mother's fit to pluck tatas and bear suckas. Sat spittin… splittin up families with no names, had no shame because it was all a part of the slave game, we didn't chose to play.

And even though our strength was merchandised, pride demoralized
Somehow our hopes and dreams managed to survive!!
And we still wonderin…..is we free yet suh….is we FREE?
NO!... too much cotton left to sow.
But if you just close your eyes….and listen to your soul, you can't help but feel the heartbeat of a million slaves dying….all over again. And regardless of how much you read…write, research, or recite…you'll always feel your ancestors bleeding… from the seeds of massa's greed. Always! But it don't matter what they write, cause they'll never know what we've known…see what we've seen… feel what we've felt.   And we'll always be wonderin' is we free yet suh?
IS WE FREE?

What's that Sound?

What's That Sound Momma?
What's that sound?
Honey, its grass growing
It's the wind blowing

It's time going on its merry way
It's the end of another day.

What's that sound Daddy?
What's that sound?
Son, its bones extending
It's brothers lending
Its time bending to meet new beginnings
It's the stretch of never ending

What's that sound grandpa?
What's that sound?
Child, that's rooster crowing
That's grandma sewing
It's the flowing of truth seeking a place to be
It's the sound of being free.

What's that sound grandma?
What's that sound?
Oh that well let me tell ya
It's hearts breaking
It's minds shaping
It's the aching of eyes filled with tears
It's the crinkle of forgotten years
It's living alone
It's finding a home
It's struggle and it's strife
Son, that sound is just the sound of LIFE.

My Color My Crime

Somewhere in a crowded mind I lost myself.
Somewhere between now and then
my past became my future.

And like rats amazed, I followed the scent
of tomorrow's cheese only to be trapped
by my own self-defeating disease.

With third eye blind, I couldn't see,
a heart untouched, I couldn't feel.
My soul silent, I had no voice
so I hid beneath my skin, denied the love within.
And watched me run from the man I could never be.

A million thoughts jaywalked inside my mind
causing traffic jams in time
but I just kept on running.

Alarms went off, sirens screamed
but I ignored the messages in my dreams
and kept right on running.

And with the stench of roadkill on its breath
time breathed death down the back of my neck.
Like minute cheetahs in hot pursuit
hunting my heritage, preying upon my pride
and I could not shake this hate.

Caught from behind I realized that
my color was not my crime.
Only time!
And I could longer hide from the man I refused to be.

The Basics of Chivalry

In addition to the aforementioned rules, gentlemen (in training) should follow these additional rules when in the presence of a lady. Chivalry may be on life support, but it is not dead yet. Be one of the few to keep this flame burning for many years to come.

Always open doors
This is perhaps the most basic rule of male etiquette out there.
It is also one of the easiest to follow so you have no reason to forget it. Whether she is about to enter your car, restaurant, club, or anyplace with a door, you should always hold it open. If there are many doors, then hold them open one after the other.

Put on her coat
Always help a lady put on her coat or jacket. This is a simple but powerful gesture.

Help with her seat
If an unaccompanied lady is sitting next to you, it is important that you help her be seated by pulling her chair out for her and gently pushing it back into place, with the lady seated of course.

Do not laugh at others' mistakes
This is perhaps one of the cruelest things one can do. When you mess up, the last thing you want is for someone not only to bring it to your attention, but to ridicule you on top of that.

Remove your hat indoors
This rule seems to have gone out the window these days. You should remove your headwear upon entering a building. Furthermore, never keep your hat on while at the dinner table. It reflects very poor etiquette.

Wait for seating before eating
When sitting down for a meal, you should wait until all the guests are properly seated and ready to commence the meal before eating. Everyone should start dining at the same time; this is a subtle but very important rule.

Greetings Folks Mike Guinn here...
I would be honored to be a featured speaker, presenter, or workshop facilitator at your next conference, or book club. I promise a uniquely powerful experience guaranteed to compliment any occasion. Thank you so much and enjoy the rest of the book.

Beautiful

Yesterday I shook hands with a crack addict and she
stole my fingerprints. Just a young girl in a bad
world with bee stings for nipples and mosquito bites
for needle tracks. And the way she wears her
 clothes just so makes her
the tiniest woman on the streets. She eats... Foreskin for
din-din and still there she be...standing on the
corner. She be like mice scrambling to hide when
the light comes on. Scrambling to hide from the sun.

It's 95 degrees in the shade and she's trying to get paid but no money she's made
today. No money she's made. And nothing pisses me off more than to see sistahs with
fever blistahs, twisting, insisting on a ride so that they can play hide the
soldier with men old enough to be their fathers, and you want to save them but why
bother? When they rather pull cock capers for paper, because nothing will save her from
her ... but her.

Armed with AZT, morphine, and dreams she be lean and mean... she be
flying, trying to find peace in back alleys the only way she knows.
But I suppose there's no hope because the only way she can cope is to tear down the
temple of her body and let it become a valley for viruses and dope.

But if only she knew just how beautiful she be!
If only she'd just kick off those high-heeled blues and choose not to lose her way. Choose
not to waste her day..... Because life is too high a price to pay.

But she'd rather be dressed in leather…. Oh so clever
She be dressed to impress… she be the best at making less look like more
She be what she chooses, confusing losing her dignity and spiritual
virginity to men who see nothing more than a whore.

But she ... doesn't have to be a midnight princess straddling fences,
bending, pretending that this is her mission in life, to lose all she was and will be in the
kneeling position. Because this is not what God intended.. It's not!

And she doesn't have to be feigning, screaming from the semen forever
choking her dreams… She doesn't. If only she'd realize that she ….is
beautiful, beautiful… just beautiful, beautiful… so beautiful... beautiful.

That her knees are not meant for concrete defeat
That her lips are not suppose to be that dry …
And if she'll just stand... take God's hand … She'll know…
And if she just slows down when she strolls past that convenience store
window… she'll know… and she'll see that she is beautiful, beautiful just
beautiful, beautiful… so beautiful... beautiful she can be.

TRIBUTE

Of winter's Frost and Robert
and Whitman waltzing by.
For Baldwin bolting forward
and Anne's Frank reply.

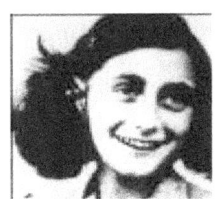

Of Langston's hue and brilliance
and Gwendolyn's bubbling brook.
For Zora's bright resilience
and the mountain Martin took.

For Rosa's spiritual spark
and Medgar's lasting evers.
From Emily's post remarks
we move on to great endeavors.

For Edgar's night we seek
and Elliot's cool review.
Of Dante's poetic peaks
near valleys Shakespeare knew.

For all the love they shared
and all the life they gave.
We pay tribute with our words
for the souls their poetry saved.

The Poets

Hands of Time

      Lying here next to never
        I become mesmerized, hypnotized
          as I watch ceiling fans
            fan the seconds
        that,
          fan the moments
        that,
            blow the hands of time

  Old moments transform into midnight scented metaphors
  surrounded by a presidium of cerulean blue
And as night waves crash into day shores,
sound becomes an epiphany that moves
through me like ripples on water,
sending messages primitive to my now

    But I am that ripple
   I am an endless reflection
     scratching,
       clawing,
         crawling,
           like some irritated beggar
             searching for answers in dumpsters,
                finding only crumbs in the rubble of life's debris

Watching,
    as life becomes this moment
        that stretches its arms into the next day
          and the next
             and the next
                until its pitched black eyes
                    become dim lit spaces
              etched in patches of day
              that float on forever and ever and ever
         Still, all I do is stand here
     watching, as ceiling fans
   fan the seconds
that,
  fan the moments
that,
  blow the hands of time

Daddy's Little Girl

Twice on Sundays and every other Monday were fun days for a father who never bothered to father... until he was bothered. Oh, he loved his children...especially Sarah.

One night from beneath the shadows of my blanket, I watched daddy tiptoe into my sister's room, like a thief, to pluck the forbidden fruit of her undeveloped flower.
She... was only ten.
I guess the taste of giggles were so much sweeter when snatched from the womb of a child too young to know that daddy was the enemy.

I watched him suck smiles fresh as lambs milk from nipples not yet ripe enough, but just right enough...for the slaughter.
And soon...she was wearing his hands, tasting his teeth...feeling the sweat drip from his chin and mix with the tears running down her cheeks.

Oh his assault was soooooo gentle and as I watched, petrified, she reached out to me with those eyes and I cried because there was nothing I could do... And as he pounded and pounded away at her essence, I just covered my head...because I was just so afraid.

And no matter how loud she screamed...and begged..NO, DADDY! NO! his pounding did not stop. He just covered her mouth one hand, spit in the otha and said...daddy luvs ya baby... and this is OUR LITTLE SECRET

For me, there will never be a sound louder than the pounding of teardrops on cold hardwood floors. And... In my eyes...there will never be a crack wider than the crease in between sheets behind closed doors.

And I think it's so messed up that nothing will ever reverse an act so perverse that even the shadows curse. Her muffled moans became an anthem of screams that haunt me to this day, because daddy stole her innocence and took our childhood away.

Sarah never speaks about those days, she doesn't have too, but I can see it in her eyes, hear it in her voice, feel it when we hug.

And sometimes …while standing near the pain of our past…next to the promise of our future, we've tried to imagine a better tomorrow… but the pounding never stops, not for her, not for me. I was just six, but I can still see daddy's tooth pick lying next to a smoldering cigarette, a sinful reminder of the flame slowly dying inside her eyes.

Sarah don't smile no more…because too heavy are scars left from life-wars now bitter memories stored in old pickle jars.

Now she's a stripper named Candy but there's nothing sweet about those hours he devoured. And as I nurse the fat lip of my shattered perception, I've wondered… what kind of man would I've become? If Daddy was the father he was suppose to be for his son?

But I suppose…I'll always be that frightened little boy… watching… and she will always be…Daddy's Little Girl.

Love Me Knots
A Poem for Destiny Bright-Eyes

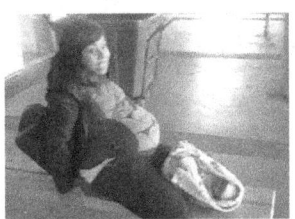

I was a county worker when I found her living in a crack house with her mother in Dallas, Texas. She was eleven going on thirty, flirty, dirty, and pregnant with HIV.   Her mother was just 16 when she had her…and her mother was only 15 when she had her. That vicious cycle, unbroken… remains.

Momma was too caught up to bring up the issue of protection, and now every time she screams, dust mites gather to hold pep rallies on her dreams. Cause for her... Life "IS" what it seems. Just a ragged bouquet of Love Me Knots.

And soon there'll be no more cartoons, only buffoons, drooling from the lust for young meat. Soon there'll be no more cotton candy, only brandy, bologna and phonies sniffing at this young pony. Drip, drop drip … she slips undercover, where mother's lover discovers her trembling from anticipation, waiting on penetration
because all she's EVER known…is full-blown DEGRADATION!

It's so sad that HIV was the only positive thing that ever happened to her. And it's too damn bad that at eleven she was molested, disrespected, unprotected, left neglected, rejected, more than her body was infected.

And the sting of being sold to men so that momma could feed her sin still burns inside me… It burns…
Who told them to love her that way….steal her day… say she could stay in that goddamned house… Where prostitution… was resolution for the pollution of her soul.   Somebody tell me WHO?

And if momma would've just followed the needle tracks back to her past, her daughter would not be just a piece of ass for cash. If she'd just said HELL NO to heathens breathing down her daughter's tender innocence, the cycle would've been broken.

I can change momma said… I can change… Fa sho...Momma, Fa sho…but there's no
change a coming just the humming of addict getting her next fix with the trix from her daughter's well-learned insolence…. And she's sooooo proud.

But there'll be no Coltrane for this child, only miles of dizzy holidays,
daisy dukes and Doobie brothers, smothering hopes with smoke and pokes,
all for momma's dope.

I can still see momma shooting up… while vagabonds violate her daughter with viruses... She's tried so hard to resist but has learned all too well how to please and tease…on her knees and live with this disease daily.

Well, .her child…was still born…and she …died… at 14…full blown…
I can still see her name chiseled on that tombstone. Destiny Bright Eyes, 1982 - 1996.

It's the reason why I write…the reason why I fight…the reason why I cry….late at night…
because she'll never read poetry. She never had a chance to be…
Hush little suga…please don't cry… Momma just wanted to get REAL HIGH.

Paralyzed

You told me, "One day God will reveal who we truly are..."
Those words may as well have been machetes slicing my heart into tiny
pieces
of unforgettable moments, that will forever leave me puzzled, paranoid,
and lonely.

My dreams are now one way corridors leading to closets packed full of
Skeletons that leave me...paralyzed from the eyes down.

Now.. I find myself faced with skeletons you've embraced and together
with lust and lies they manipulate faith, leaving nothing but this empty
space.

And I... am overcome by numbness because the sum of us– we = none.
I wish I could add up all the times I'd wished I'd said something, done
something, prayed for something instead of just standing there, staring
into that closet watching your skeletons devour our love.

But I just stood there... PARALYZED...
Dodging the dilation of your speechless eyes, as each wink became an
exclamation, with no explanation for why you refused to STAY!

Because my tears could fill the Atlantic.
And there is not now nor will there ever be a universe that could ever hope
to hold all the love I still have in my heart for you.

Dodging the dilation of your speechless eyes, as each wink became an
exclamation, with no explanation for why you refused to STAY!

STAY... for all the times our lips met and...
STAY! For all the laughter we'll never forget. The road trips...the parks,
the poetry from our hearts...Baby...Please...STAY
Because...You are my poetry.

And if you truly knew you the way I do then you'd know why I'd get on my
hands and knees, reach inside my soul...gather moonbeams and
starlight... Arrange them in a beautiful bouquet, place them at your feet
and say... I GREW THESE FOR YOU.

And if you were here... right now.. I'd mix teardrops into paints and cry
rainbows... then I'd capture each one on canvas and create a picture that says
just 3 words... I LOVE YOU!
"One day God WILL reveal who we truly are"
And maybe in the next lifetime when roses are blue, our spirits are new, us = me
and you. You'll allow me to be your poetry. But for now... Even your skeletons
have frowns... Because, without you... I'll always be paralyzed... from the eyes down...

The Heart of a Man Who Screams

On hot days… I can still see Jesus standing near the dumpster…crying, As old roaches became bold roaches, scattering from inside the blood soaked diapers…of a Nubian newborn… left lying in a morgue of moments.
Cause of death; Scoliosis of the soul and Spiritual Spina Bifida!
His back, blue, eyes black, skin puffy and swollen like a brown bag of rainbows. And I… remember kneeling in the vomit of vowels, swatting flies, searching for signs of poetry in his eyes, but all I found...was an obituary of ancient welts scribbled in a eulogy of bruises. And as the last gasp oozed from between his lips, it was as if all the insects in the world had assembled there.

And it... took... everything I had to keep from picking him up and cradling him my arms. And no matter how detailed the gathering of evidence…or how thorough the autopsy…FORENSICS …would NEVER find the fingerprints that stopped his beating heart. And that day, my heart became the heart of a man who screams.
On HOT DAYS! Like today, I'm reminded that… to his mother, he was a buffaloed soldier whose arms and legs became brittle like little hot wings at a picnic for maternal regrets. And every year, EVERY YEAR!
I've tried to write a poem to stop the dying.

And every day, I've tried to resuscitate his soul with my own.
And EVERY NIGHT, when I can't sleep, I've counted the roaches running from his diapers like sheep, re-living that moment, over and OVER AGAIN! before waking in a pool of sweat…trying my best to breathe my life into his chest. Look…LOOK!… see I still have scars on my tongue from his seizures, gone blind from life and lies, struggled to revive the light in his eyes with mine.

And every time I've tried to save him…it's always too damn late.

Because SOMEONE had already pulled the shade on his sun, painted his rainbows black, and colored the moon blue. And no matter what I do. Nothing will EVER put back the Cherokee in his cheeks, reverse the rigamortus in his smile or take away this artistic arthritis. Nothing!

And some nights… I cry so hard that my tears… become crystal midgets migrating back to Africa like passion's poetic pygmies. And no matter how much I open, release, breathe. Open, release, BREATHE! He…will never live again. NEVER!

And I'm dying here. Lord, I'm DYING. And I WISH with my last breath, for either a genie or a JESUS, or some kind of magic and not just tragic hours of praying, hoping someone up there is listening.

And if there is a heaven, I hope he's in it. All mended.
So that I can stop counting the stars he'll never see and be the man I need to be. And right now…right here. I'll deliver this poem as if it were the King of prayers from the heart of a man who screams.

LITTLE WINKY

My name is little Winky

I fell down and hurt my Pinky

But I got right up

No Tears! No Fuss

But I think I made a STINKY!!

(Unknown Artist)

Bastard

I was born a bastard. That's what you told me Mamma. Dark moon of your nightmare...half and half but not whole of a sum from a story told over and over again from the center of my soul.

I was just 3 minutes removed from being torn from the uterus of then way back when the sun turned its back and shadows cried. And even though just a seed I could still feel you bleed from daddy's dirty deed...BUT HE WAS THE BASTARD Mama...not me.

I remember swimming inside you as you lay near death...and when you were well enough to feel my moment...your anger and resentment rumbled like thunder and I wondered how much longer I had to be before...You got rid of me. And even though an unwanted fetus I knew who I was...

YOUR SON! The un-chosen one.

And in the ovum of that moment...I felt you concede my existence... no longer resisting the urge to murder the unborn metaphor and leaving me lying in a pool of aborted promises. And that day was the day I learned to escape danger by dodging coat hangers jabbing with the anger of the desperate stranger you'd become. That day...I felt you scraping and screaming as you squatted to be free of me. And you almost did mama.

But I...hung on...And as blood ran thick and hot scalding the essence of your innocent...it left me clinging to your womb like a dangling participle clutching a poem yet written. But I survived Mama, I survived to prove that statistics are just bullshit and

I am nobody's goddamn misfit...and I can still hear your screaming...
"BOY, YOU AIN'T GON' BE SHIT"!
But I am. And I will no longer be a pawn for food stamps and income tax, cause I am more than that...I am more. I am more than just sperm jettisoned from the tomb of my father's already limp dick...I am fucking more than that...I am more. Still ...you said I was born a bastard. So this poem is for all those years you beat me for looking like him...

And this line is the tie that binds me to the umbilical of those nights you made me feel like a weed without roots at the foot of an empty tree...cause no one was there...just me. But I...am not like my father, Mama. I am living proof that flowers can bloom from deceit. I am not like my father, Mama...

Because 1% of you inside me is the reason why I believe.

And we've...come a long way from belt buckles and criticism...
And I just want you to know that the only love I even knew, grew to create me... from you. So I'm gonna take all the power and all this rage and leave a part of soul on the national stage...for you. Because I am not a bastard, Mama I'm A POET! And one day my metaphors will open heaven doors and leave tear prints across the sky. And that day...that glorious, wonderful day...you and I...will soar...Love ya Mama

A Poet

I must be getting closer to finding my soul mate. Because lately, all I see is her image in my dreams. You know that special someone who compliments my swerve with her verbs fills my mind with her words, defies gravity with her curves. A Poet.

Someone whose love becomes voodoo and the way I do everything from writing her name to playing games is simply taboo. The kind of woman who makes me feel so warm inside that I just want to get butt naked, run outside, and try to capture the sunshine falling from her eyes. Someone who knows how to celebrate satisfaction with a reaction from her soul and understands… That her mission is not to put me in a position to make up things she wished I'd done one too many sins ago. Someone who knows just how to flow. Ya know. And each morning when I wake beside her. She'll know just how much I care. Because it will show… in the curl of her toes, the crease in her clothes, the kiss on her nose. And it won't even matter that she has that…morning breath, because her breath is my morning.

You see, I'm a dreamer. A man who just wants to share his heart with her heart, his spirit with her spirit, leave tear prints in the shape of ankhs so that her soul can hear it.

And at night while she's laughing, crafting izms from the day, I'll cry my way back inside her eyes until her smile becomes my religion. And don't cha think, I deserve to have someone who won't run from the warmth of my sun? Someone who allows my will to give in to the pen in her hands as

I become a man in the corner of her eyes and then die right there, over and over again until we get it right. Someone who enjoys writing my love into her life, because I'm her favorite poem. And she can't help the way she feels she can't stop the way she is and why would she?

And all I need to know right now is. IS THERE A POET IN THE HOUSE
TONIGHT??   STAND UP!! Stand…take my hand and together you and I. We'll write rhythm, read rhymes, and make little baby wisdoms from the knowledge of just knowing what love is.

You see I'll always feel this way. Because in your hands, I'll place my hands and then our hands will become one hand holding on to forever. And whenever you need me, you won't have to look far, just glance left of moonlight, right of a falling star and there I'll be, waiting for your chills to catch up with the wave of Goosebumps flying south towards the summer of my kisses. And I'll always be there, not far from here where love first began as tight ass line, written in a love poem scribbled on a napkin, abandoned at the back table at our favorite restaurant, somewhere near the sweet-n-low and heaven.

You see I've always felt this way… a rhythm searching for rhymes, that poem inside your mind, in love 'til the end of time.

The Blackest Child

Weeping softly they wonder why, their mothers cry, and Fathers deny? Why are they only allowed to make small steps, or take little sips from a cup of life that overflows with denial, never quenching the smile of the loneliest child?

Walking slowly, little girls and boys, sapped of love, devoid of joy Hardened to the touch, missing so much, hugs and kisses making desperate wishes, for a home that for a while shelters the heart of a battered child.

Wading slightly in ponds of tears, naked emotions swim in lakes of fears, because hope's ocean never appears. So, they sail seas of misery, searching as far as sad eyes can see. But with no oar to row, no place to go no land in sight day or night, rare tides of smiles elude for awhile the salty lips of an abandoned child.

Wanting silence from the pain seeking shelter from life's hard rain, as it beats their brow. Lord, help them now to see their way by the light of your day Hoping soon that your bright moon still shines, please let's help find the mythical smiles of the Blackest Child.

Where Souls Grow

This is the house that slams built.
And I'm here to put poetry back in spoken word because what we do is a gift. So with you permission, I'd like to audition for your heart tonight. You see... it's time to push all the bullspit aside, stop pimpin' pride, conquer, and divide.
Because this ain't no place for egos.
Here... souls grow. Let me break it down to ya!

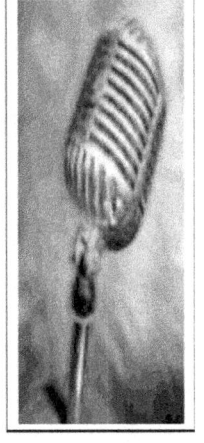

Poetry begins and ends from within and you can't run from it ... You have to become it. By taking a pen and letting it blend into an extension of your heart. Then annunciate with conviction, punctuate your inflictions with diction. Cause you got to feel, reveal, and most of all, keep it real.

The bounce, pronounce, SQUEEEEEEZE every ounce of sound into pronouns profound than LIFE!. Then you got to write. Put your back into it and WRITE! Sharpen your skills and write. Till it becomes a place for your voice in the sky. And if you have to, Cry, bleed, die... so that you can be reborn on the inside.

Now this ain't no easy task. You gonna have to practice. Sacrifice night and day and PRACTICE. Revise compromise and PRACTICE. Till you can recite life in your sleep. Cause then and ONLY then, will you be ready and when you are... They'll know it; your performance will show it. With an explosion of emotions wrapped in an ocean of rhythms. That's when you transform. Use your breath body and arms. Defy the norms and become the best damn Poem!

You got to jump up on tables, forget labels in America, we're able to spit this uncensored writ like Dave Chappelle on cable.

You gotta move your hands like this and say something poetic like.
"POETRY ISN'T SOMETHING I DO, IT'S WHAT I AM..." And damn it I am.
And this is how you slam. Listen... you got to conceive it, to achieve it, and then be it.
Let it flow... because here... Chills hug goose bumps.
We drop bombs like Don Juan, get mean like Janean, spit the fax to the MAX!
Ain't no time to relax.

You see, it's a thin blue line between depression and rainbows... But you know what? You got to keep on 'slangin.' Banging out that verse, 'til poetry becomes a curse that makes spoken-word rookies rehearse. You see, there's no brighter light than the light of a poet. Escrible.. Por los ninos y los Dios. Right Natasha Carrizosa?

You see this knowledge was conceived in the fallopian of an Ethiopian.
And I ain't got time for tantrums and silly ass moping. Cause I'm hoping to remain a fixture on the spoken-word scene. Cause I'm back where I belong wiser and lean.
And to you spoken-word thieves I'm droppin' words like rockets and yes, its true I have deep pockets. You see... I'm leaving all of me right here. Cause this is the house that poetry built. And I ain't got time for egos ... Because tonight.
MY SOUL GROWS

Africa

On sacred ground I stand
My arms stretched out to heaven
As roots gather strength from the quilt of day

Listen!

Africa's song is playing softly in the distance
As evening breezes sing melodies off key

The wind blowing, becomes my breath
Stars shining become my eyes
And I become one with the setting sun
Quietly, I watch day tease night

As it plays tag with dragon flies
While rolling clouds rush to discuss my astrology

Like stolen pieces of memory, time descends from tree tops
As free-falling reminders of days gone by

A restless summer nestles in the yawn of nature's bosom
While heavenly sheets of autumn, blanket the earth
With foliage spread from the breeze, of pre-winter's scorn

Spiritual alchemy rises from burial grounds of seasons before
Yesterday, becomes an eyewitness to misty colored memories,
Bolting downward in assault of spiraling song

Listen!

Cleopatra is laughing in colors again
Creating sons in the image of my reality

Listen!
Mother nature is weeping destiny upon dreams
Caressing souls, leaving tear-prints upon the
Cheeks of another season

Now, bare feet make sun-tracks across the sky
Casting shadows that become moon-bows of hope

As time chases life and life chase me

Candlelight Reminds Me

Every time I light a candle.

Whiskey scented memories begin to burn
inside, filling my mind with the scent of you.

And as I close my eyes
I think of those milky white moments
and the moon smiles with me.

I remember nights when two went into one, and one
Between two.
Mathematically we fit like two square roots
multiplied to infinity.
And it was just 9 past 6, when I found you trembling
there.

A mixture of night and laughter
exploded into rush of tears and I cried too
remember…

But it's OK to cry,
because I'm here and I won't stop.

I won't ever stop!

Until it's time to re-light the candles
inside you.

We Miss You

In Loving Memory of Colleta Brown-Sheppard

*In our dreams we see an empty chair
where once you were there.*

And we miss you!

*In our eyes there's a place near the sun where we run to you,
come to you, just to hold on to you..*

And we miss you!

*In our hearts there's a space so cold that shadows cry from the loneliness
of you not being there.*

And we miss you grandpa!

*And if you were here we'd tell you that all the love we ever knew
grew to create us from you.*

*We'd sing to you our song, hold out our palms and wait for your smile to
come.
Your voice so soft spoken was a token of your kindness and we'll always
find this to be sweetest memory we've ever known.
And one day, our prayers will open heaven's doors and leave tear prints
across the sky.
And one day, the love you shared, the way you cared, just being
there will rise up so high...
That on that day... that glorious wonderful day... you will forever
 soar inside our eyes.*

Because we miss you... Grandma and we love you always...

From Your Loving Family

Love's Jambalaya

A Recipe For A Successful Relationship

Begin With A Big Bowl Of Openness
4 cups Love
5 tablespoons Patience
2 cups Understanding
3 tablespoons Tenderness
1 cup Forgiveness
1 gallon Faith
2 cups Friendship
A barrel of Fun
1 teaspoon Laughter
1 cup Romance
A smidgen of spontaneity
A pinch of Trust

First you combine love and understanding
Mix thoroughly with tenderness
Add Faith and Trust
Then blend in friendship, forgiveness and
"please" be patience
Next, stir in romance and have fun with it
Sprinkle with laughter and spontaneity
Then bake with sunshine, let cool by moonlight
Serve daily in a dish of passion.

On the Wings of Destiny

Your journey has begun and now it's time to ride
upon the wings of destiny.

Forever may your spirit soar,
Your mind explore,
Your eyes peek,
Your heart seek.

May your soul be saved,
Your mind behave,
Your wishes come true.

May you find…

…YOU.

A Thousand Tomorrows

Desire burns at the tip of your tongue
                            and sizzles
                                    on your lips
                                              like the sun.

The heat
      from your smile
            could melt the coldest moment.

            The warmth of your touch
                  could soothe the roughest of times

But that fire
    inside your eyes
        could ignite a thousand tomorrows...and one heart...
                                                    mine

        May the candles that light your path

                Be the flame that guides your spirit forever.

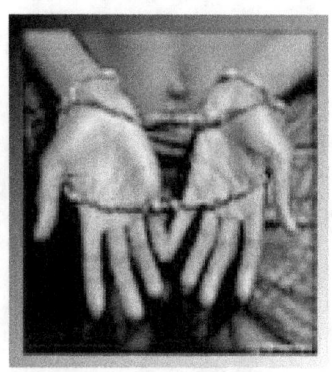

That Island in Your Eyes

*Love is the essence of my domain and it contains
All that I was and will be as I am and always will be in love.*

*But like ice melting
Tears flow in Rapids from my eyes
Flooding my aching heart.*

*The thaw from frozen emotions
Create waterfalls within
Without you I don't know where I begin.*

Tell Me!

*What have you done leaving me blue?
Loving no one....Needing you!*

*What do I do now?
PLEASE ... HEAR MY CRIES!*

*I'm stranded ... All Alone ..."On That Island In Your Eyes"
My heart beats a tempo soft and slow,
like sad songs playing on the radio
Your kisses forsake me
Your smile eludes
Your hugs... once snug...for me... no longer choose.*

*So I'm saying hello again... to sad good-byes...
Stranded all alone on that ISLAND IN YOUR EYES!*

Mourning

Syllables and foul vowels

scratch a trail

along my heart

like an etch-a-sketch

tracing the peaks of yesterday.

A litany of creative gestures

linger in echoes of then

leaving mouths agape

but voice is denied exit and lovers are

left to dye in shades of blue.

Beaches of sandy predilection

erode from a constant pounding

simply ill-prepared for the relentless tide

of words crashing against its shore

leaving love weakened by storms refusing to subside.

Centric

Transient circles
*   of night and day,*
*   become a circumference of green earth*
*   diluted by shades of blue sky.*
*   Eternity without an identity,*
becomes lost in a kaleidoscope of black and white.

*   Eyes empty deny light*
*   flowers refuse to bloom*
*   time splits into metaphors*
*   seeps into pores*
*   seeking entry where*
darkness first began.

Skin erupts into colors
*   and a universe is born within.*
*   Gray skies speak in*
*   luminescent trilogies,*
*   raging like*
a million red rivers before.

A moment's kiss,
*   a second's bliss*
*   and an millennium*
*   blazes on in ion increments.*

*   At the blink of an eye,*
*   adventures glean*
* in tunnels of forever*
Shifting in galaxies of infinity
Life comes full circle...

*   .....and circles never end.*

In Our Heaven

"If we could capture wisdom… then this religion of indecision would not become our prison." And maybe we'd have something more to believe in.

There's a darkness still bleeding from this wound, because where I'm from has become a place with drums for children just a slum in need of rebuilding. The Ghetto

In Our Heaven…we seen no streets of gold or angels standing at crystal podiums Waiting to greet you at the pearly gates. There are no harps, or rainbows, or grand piano's…nothing beautiful…And maybe this…is why children…hoping for brighter tomorrows…keep slippin through the cracks.

To get to my Heaven, you just step through a hole in a barbed wire fence, leading to an empty playground where dead pygmies hang from monkey bars like little pot- bellied bats whose wings have been clipped by an angry God too busy to answer prayers. Near the entrance, there's a giant dumpster overflowing with the battered spirits of abandoned babies screaming for their teenage mothers… and I suppose that's where lost souls go.

Inside, a man wearing an "I love Bush" T shirt smiles like a pimp, as he checks his list for section 8 rape and motions to an rickety wooden ladder where black cats circle and grin. In the courtyard, Billie Holliday sits beneath a hanging tree with noose shaped leaves holding an empty syringe…dying…from spiritual laryngitis.

To my left…Martin stands barefoot, handcuffed…surrounded by confederate soldiers Yelling, "Ain't no dreams here **NIGGAH**", you took the wrong DAMN turn at the Mountain.

To my right…The Klan rapes Abe Lincoln, Malcolm is on his back in a straight jacket and James Byrd is still running behind that damned truck in Jasper, Texas struggling to pick up the pieces of his soul.

In Our Heaven…The police, play paint ball with the blood of black children while Osama and Jeffery Dahmer place bets. And the ancestors, just sit on stumps like black leprechauns watching… as priest turned pedophiles drool as they wait for lil' Hansels and Gretels to lose their way… and history makes damn sure they do... by leaving trails of broken promises scattered with the restless souls of a million slaves.

In Our Heaven, the bombing of the 16th Street Baptist Church is a national celebration, where heroes like Hitler and Hoover propose a toast to the ghosts of dead daughters.
And ANYONE caught believing in themselves …ANYONE…would have their spirits lynched by the rope of their own hope. Cause in my ghetto it's a sin to DREAM!

Foster homes become concentration camps for children starving for attention, and there ain't no such thing as college because knowledge is NOT the key to success.
And HERE they don't give a DAMN if you don't do your best. IT DON'T MATTER…THIS DON'T MATTER… WE DON'T MATTER…

You see…THIS is what we see in our heaven and if things don't change…
This is ALL WE'LL BE in our heaven.
This is what we believe my heaven to be. Cause in my heaven…
There IS NO TOMORROW ….just the hell of living …TODAY!!

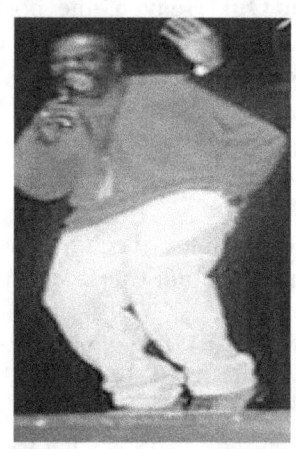

*******AMAZING ENERGY*******

Boo-ku's

Last year I lost love
And with it a part of me
Please return my heart.

Shackled ignorance
Barefeet bare witness O lord
Grant me wisdom's key.

        Yesterday is gone
        And tomorrow is present
        Where did the time go?

        Broken heart refrains
        Because no tears remain and
        Eyes refuse to cry.

        The trail from old tears
        Flowing down ebony cheeks
Leave tracks for kisses.

Blue skies in brown eyes
The bright sun rays give way to
Love on a clear day.

Within your rivers
Flow bubbling brooks of lust
How I long for sips.

Beginning of the End

Scented jasmine glisten like crimson rain
As lemon colored perceptions leap at dawn.
Lips, swollen from soulful silence
Swallow dew in a metaphor of shadows.
And all who taste bow to its rhythm
The bittersweet essence of time.

Lips, swollen from soulful silence
Swallow dew in a metaphor of shadows.
And all who taste, bow to its rhythm
The bittersweet essence of time.

As flaming moments set fire to time,
Bright lights burn in a reflection of rain.
Minutes command seconds in rhythm
As darkness withers from cremation's dawn.
Empty moments creep in hazy shadows
And time becomes a coffin of silence.

No need to fear the might of her silence
Her passion is but a reminder of time.
But even as she hides from crawling shadows
Stolen moments deny the coming rain
And peace be not still in her dawn
For midnight refuses refuge to rhythm.

But without day, there would be no rhythm
Memories would cease in silence.
Here, there, misty colored teardrops become as fresh as dawn,
Resting in fractions of time
Waiting to murder memory with black rain.
And thus begins the might of shadows.

Cautiously she stalks me in these shadows
As I bide my stride in rhythm.
Madness confines anxious rain
Using the wind and seasons as weapons of silence.
And while nightingales rest wings on hands of time
Her loathing sprouts contempt at dawn.
Here she comes again, cursing the dawn

Sister death on winged shadows.
Perhaps eternity will grant me a second chance at time
Maybe I'll be blessed with the stroke of her rhythm
But if not, I'll simply weep in silence.
Cry in colors and spew sonnets in the rain
But if not, I'll simply weep in silence.
Cry in colors and spew sonnets in the rain
As certain as dawn, succumbs to rain.
As deadly as the silence of shadows
Time will always steal my rhythm.

Conversation with an Angel
Written Especially for My Soul Mate

"Love is patient, love is kind, it beareth all things, believeth all things, hopeth all things Endureth all things. LOVE NEVER FAILS"

Good Morning Beautiful,
It's me. I'm standing at the end of your storm holding a rainbow, a ring, my heart. It's yours. I know it's not much right now... but it's all I've got.
And my only hope is that one day ... it will be enough.

You see I've been having these dreams again....about when I first met you. Remember, You were edible mahogany, a sugar-coated rhapsody, every man's fantasy. Just Beautiful.

And when you spoke to me ... hmmmm... that's when your breath became my breath, your smile became my sky and my search for a soul mate... was over.

I was so afraid for days to say anything because I knew that talking to you would be like
having a conversation with an angel and I didn't wanna do anything to mess that up...
That's why I waited so long just to say... Hello.

And right now, right here I'm on my knees, the king I wanna be...bags empty, with only one promise. NO MORE BROKEN RECORDS...
BECAUSE I AM ALL THE MAN YOU'LL EVER NEED.
JUST LET ME BE YOUR WINGS! AND SOON YOU'LL SEE...

You see I've learned to take my time when it comes to true love, to rely on faith, and the man above. Because there is no blueprint for relationships, just the heart's compass, the soul's maps and how far we go.... is entirely dependent on divine intervention.

And even though hope's hurricane never ends inside your eyes, I can still feel the winds spin within and it's the closest to HEAVEN I've ever been.
Baby, I love you now. I loved you then.
So I write this poem for you. What else would a poet in love ever do?
Yes...it's true... I've been in love since that night at 5th Avenue.

Now I know how you feel about commitments right now. ...and I know that you never asked for my affection. I respect that, I do. But one day when it stops raining inside and the thunder disappears from your eyes.
I'll be at the end of that storm holding a mold of your soul in my own.
With a rainbow, a ring, my heart and I love you...

Of Seasons Before

Mesmerized by cool reminders
shadows tumble from treetops
creeping in crimson horror
and I become a slave to dusk.

Paranoid I try to hide from autumn
but I'm too damn weak to move now
instead, my feet cling to this moment
like the leftover colors of spring,
while silence settles into summer's ashes
next to nowhere, close to never.

Tonight we become seasons,
emotions clawing at the moon
smiling east of one-way nights
crying west of morning's past
trespassing on winter's property.

So strange this moment
That tempts time with a flicker,
awaken eyes with sight newborn
so love can flourish in full bloom.

There is no why to what we do now
because becomes a reason to be
and we fall in love with the seasons all over again.

Without You

Without you

Silence is raped by thunder

lighting steals quiet from the night.

Bare feet become burdened by memories

of a fear that grabs the soul, chokes sound, denying life within

leaving clinched eyes grimacing from

painful reminders of days gone by.

Stitched lips simply refuse to speak yesterday's lies

as tongues hunt for helpful hints

cheek and teeth conspire to stifle

the truth of moments bare.

A heart is hardened by paralyzing silhouettes

unable to cope with crippling despair

I refuse to be half of a whole that has no half to hold

I can't go on this way,

I won't go on this way,

I can't go on this way without you

Shades of Day

*You awake to the sound of day,
gloom's viciously cloaked reminders.*

*Become Illusive, ghastly shadows,
Ill-tempered as tornados before.*

*Time engages in an assault of color
as life daydreams in shades of gray.*

*And the future becomes red slaughter
beckoned from Eve's fruity appetite,*

*Astute blues relent rage,
Oblique in rainy tranquility,
Sunshine sheens juicy repent,
Slothing acquiesce of rebellious rays.*

*The reluctant tolerance of blushing cheeks
beseech bold and bright compositions.*

*Till disguised in meadow green,
skunks dusk like preying mantis.
And now these shapes,
A cataclysm of insignificance,
slight the dawn of man
defying existence in tints of time.*

A Stranger in Your Eyes

Minutes, hours, day pass
But that look I'm so used to, refuses to return to your eyes

Evolutions revolve in revolutions of unresolved resolutions
But time is the selfish keeper of what used to be a symphony
Poetic revelations be told in cool beats
Smooth like fat grooves no longer lean
My soul in a song

And even though, the shadow from my blackness
cast silhouettes all over the room
you are still so un-aware
That I'm. ...even ...there

In your absence I've become engulfed by a revolution
of silence
Swallowed by the night
Lost in this moment

A prisoner to a memory
I'm just a slave to love's cliché

Passion refuses to caress ebony with its touch
Whispers curse the notion
As black rain drips blue pain
leaving yesterday's tear-prints on my now
and my heart becomes a place without light

I no longer want to taste your hyphenated kisses
I refuse to respond exponentially
to the undeserving swerve of your smile
How dare you do me this way?

Mystics guess and psychics confess
That they cannot see me in your future
and this prediction sheds light on the rhythm in your lies
And I see you for the first time

Oh if only it were not so
But I see you now
I see a stranger inside your eyes

Shattered Glass

Beauty of raindrops
the essence of snow tops
The strength of time

Melancholy lament is captured in an opus of
echoes and box springs
Whispers of bitter sweet drama from the night before

Mockery of smiles and smirks
Gesturing cool commands
As moans lie hidden in winter's pillow

Secrets become pieces of
broken glass
Which the breath of life has
passed through
and left shattered in a
million requiems
Falling
Fading
Breaking
Refusing to grow
To breathe
To sing
To dream.

Through Ghetto Eyes

I see life... through Ghetto eyes
and speak from a ghetto heart.
My Shadow is... my only disguise
All I am... the ghetto -- is a part.

Through ghetto eyes---I've seen
Young mothers... battered and gray.
And fatherless homes,,, they left to roam
Because of fear --- they couldn't stay.

Through ghetto eyes…I've witnessed
Gunsmoke fill the air.
And on cold floors, behind closed doors
The dead --- mirror my stare.

With ghetto ears... I've listened
To grandma's desperate plea
For respect to be respected and no longer rejected
by the young whose spirit's run free.

Through ghetto eyes... I remember...
Block parties no fights or fuss
A time of love no pushing, no shoves
And your neighbor... you could trust.

With ghetto eyes... I've glared...
through windows --- barred with pain.
And watched fathers, mothers, sisters, and brothers
Trade pride for government gain.

These ghetto lashes have left deep gashes
that scarred, disfigured, and maimed.
But I've had to take pride of the ghetto inside
So ghetto memories... are not all... that remained.

Blue Interludes

Confined between sheets of song,
Music spills lyrics like liquid spirit absorbing chills.
Even then no masterpiece becomes of my separated self.
Stale lines steal minutes from my life as a familiar form takes shape,
distracting me from my task with incessant banging and clanging on the
bars of her paper cage.

The ink destroys and recreates my thoughts
as wills collide in a fight for survival-
hers for release from a shallow prison of pages
mine for the return of my sanity and
relief from the chaos she wages.

As minutes become hours, I press on knowing I must prevail.
Words distort themselves into a cryptic smear
seen through the sting of my tearful stare.
Approaching desperation, I write without care for rhythm or form.

The reflections pouring from my pen reveal
nothing of what rages within.
An arsenal of emotions attack from every side-
wrath, loss, shame, and pain conspire against my serenity.
Still there are others I cannot own for fear
they will consume what remains of my identity.

This night I envy those who sleep in
peaceful oblivion to my torment.
Would that I could enter dreams where
steps of faith do not lead to disappointment.

Exiled captives scream unsettling tidings
demanding to be dealt with outside the bounds of this paper cage.

A LETTER TO MY BROTHER
To My Brother Jr.

Yes, it's been years. But it is not because of your IQ. And it's not because I think you are a DUMB DUMB. It has been mainly because I was so disappointed when you made yet another STUPID mistake of getting locked up AGAIN!

SO I vowed to cut you off for a while so that you could really see how much you hurt us by not being MAN ENOUGH TO STAY YO ASS OUTTA JAIL.

You had a good job and apartment but it wasn't enough for you.
Drugs and stealing and choosing the wrong people. Bad choices, bad women, letting people use you. I was glad to see you locked up … because you weren't smart enough to realize what a blessing it was to be FREE!

I guess you don't care nothing about FREEDOM HUH?
Thousands of people died so that you could be free and you blew it…
So, how dare you try that weak ass guilt trip on me?
Oh, so now you need some extra money and I'm supposed to feel guilty and send you some money? That's a bunch of BS big bro.

I love you… I swear I do… but you have got to kick your drug habit outside and be a man for the first time in your life.
Tell me why you keep stupid mistakes and getting locked up?

Because if you didn't, then we wouldn't be having this conversation right now. WOULD WE? I'm coming to see you. Put me on the list and tell Mark to do the same. Both of y'all gon mess around and never see Mom and Dad alive again.
I guess you don't care enough about them to keep yo ass out of jail either do you?

I've been going through hell. Shot twice in an attempted carjacking, run over by a drunk driver, lost my job and had 15 warrants and had to go to jail for a while my damn self, so don't you dare think that you the only one in prison.

Life is a prison when you are not being a man about yours… And I just got out myself. 5 years I've been running and hiding. Education and smarts don't mean nothing… if you make bad choices. I've slowed down now. Got me a good woman and a good job and my license back… HELL, I got my life back.
And I ain't about to lose it again. Now that I don't have any warrants. I can come and see you. I will send you 20 dollars just tell me where and keep the letters coming. I love ya, Big Brother... JR we all do…..

Michael Guinn your little bro….

Shallow the Water

    Standing in a pool of tears

    I question my feeble existence.

  Often it is this weakness

that denies me life.

Stillness cries out in waves

 As tears force emotions to compliment the mood.

 Waters rise meter by moon

  Essence becomes a prisoner of circles

  And now eyes become rivers run dry.

 Life is captured by time

 held hostage by night

 consumed by sound

 Just a moment that quickly fades away

   Now my revolution, denied

   Evolution, declined

   Reincarnation becomes my soul's resilience

   And shallow waters are shallow no more

May I

May I be your Midnight in shining Armor?
Rescue you from emotional distress.
Aid in your escape from lonely dungeons.
May I?

Please
Let me slay that dragon inside your heart
with just one soft kiss...
and make your soul the castle of my deepest affection
May I?

And if you'll
just come with me tonight my queen
I promise that the thunder you'll feel
will not stop until the sun returns to your eyes

So please ...

May I?

An Angel's Halo

There's a place just left of the rising sun
Where women and theology linger
Wearing hats in shapes of more than one
Fixed with delicate fingers

Nestled in bright congregations of color
Against clouds of cotton moments
Beseeched with blackness big and bolder
Their splendor pay boastful homage

Proud crowns, perched upon brown
Illuminate the day with style
Like the brilliance of colorful sound
Shades of red, in shadows of now

What a site to see, come shouts of glee
As the preacher turns to thee
"Sistah I sho do like that hat"
Grinning, from chin to knee

Their beauty shrouds day with wisdom
Mesmerizing time with light
Like an Angel's Halo, its blessed vision
Brings the wonder of miracles and might

Saints whisper gossip at the skies
While truth sermons sizzle at the brim
And heavenly melodies weep from eyes
Wrapped in tears of swaddling hymns
"Cause Sistah I Sho Do Like that Hat"

The Color of Misty Blues

Tangled in a cornucopia of song
Horns blow a breath of fresh air
Like Billie crying colors of misty blues
That breath was "YOU."

You be that shade of night
Dark as jazz shadows against the moon
Teasing time with pieces of a dream

Girl you are so "saxxy"
Your smile is like a sudden rush of music
Sung in tones of astrology
Like a century of forbidden whispers.

And the setting sun simply delights like slaves
freed from a summer of trumpets when you're near
Baby, the rain that falls here, begins and ends in your eyes
It begins and ends with you.

If only there were a way to capture night or
corral the day.
Night and day would belong to you
And music, would collide with echoes in the wind
Like the color of Misty Blues.

Finding Your Own Voice

Teaching Teens and Young Adults Respect for Self and Others
By Michael Guinn-MSW

Greetings: My name is Michael Guinn, founder of Fort Worth Slams, which is a program that utilizes creative writing, role playing and motivational speaking to effect social change. We offer an intensely provocative workshop that includes expert assistance on building higher self-esteem, self-awareness, and social relevancy through very unique and creative methods. This is a creative attempt to model appropriate social behavior by making teens more aware of how detrimental destructive behavior can be to their future.

TOUGH TIMES, TOUGH KIDS, TOUGH METHODS

Let us share our knowledge and experience in a fusion of interpersonal communication tactics that are fun, engaging, and educational. The first step is to establish rapport and from that we build TRUST which will help us help your youth to open up and share. From that we'll incorporate techniques that instill pride in self and respect for others! This workshop includes free materials and one-on-one consultation that is intensely personal and REAL. You tried your way... now TRY IT OUR WAY! All you have to do allow us to share our experience, heart, and soul.

This is a unique hands-on approach to addressing behavioral, academic, social and spiritual issues that hinder our children's growth and understanding. If we improve concentration, then they are able to listen. If they are listening, then we can teach. And what we teach is Social responsibility, Academic accountability, and most importantly, RESPECT FOR SELF AND OTHERS. This program has been successful in decreasing bad language, bad grades, drug use, teen pregnancy, STDs, smoking, disrespectful behavior (sagging etc.)

This innovative speaker/presenter series is excellent for specialized events, i.e.: libraries, any youth event, workshops, freshman orientations, alumni events, graduations, or as a way of bringing social awareness to your facility. Our work with youth has been deemed emotionally therapeutic and spiritually edifying by women's groups, rehab centers, juvenile detention facilities, church conventions, substance abuse clinics, HIV and STD prevention coalitions and any group interested in using **EVERYTHING** at their disposal to effect social change. We've been champions for positive social change for years.

THIS PRESENTATION IS ALSO IDEAL FOR HIGH SCHOOLS, COLLEGES, REVIVALS, RECREATION CENTERS, SUMMER YOUTH CAMPS, CONVENTIONS, PERFORMING ARTS CENTERS, THEATERS AND SUPPORT GROUPS. Academic Programs that could benefit:

- Broadcast Journalism majors
- English majors
- English Education majors
- Theatre Arts majors
- Social Work and Sociology majors
- Criminal Justice majors
- Nursing majors
- Human Behavior majors.

Allow me to inspire and enlighten. **YOU WILL NOT BE DISSAPOINTED**

Sometimes we all Cry In Colors

***Book This Amazing Speaker for
Your next conference, symposium
school assembly, Beautillion, Cotillion
Jazz set, wedding, girl's night out,
family reunion, class reunion,
Afterschool program or college event.***

Trails of Tears

Indian nation of thousands proudly roamed
Across North Texas plains they called their own.
Lived life to the fullest, happy and free
On wide-open range as far as the eye could see.

Buffalo hunts from morning till noon
At night, old wolves howled at the moon.
On Trinity's banks they'd fish and swim
Rode bareback on mustang wild as the wind.

The laughter of children, pride and joy of a tribe.
A time before warriors had to run or hide
Mixed signals of smoke sent out a
warning.
They'll be coming for your gold in the
morning.

Peace pipe stuffed with wacky tobacky
Clouded the vision of "Chief me happy."
Tricked into treaties, written as jokes
Burnt teepee hopes, went up in smoke.

Greedy soldiers in gray patrolled the range
Fought with natives resistant to change.
Wichita scattered, as Comanche'd flee
Birth of Fort Worth when Texas was three.

Forced west to find new homes
To rocky hills dry as a bone.

Innocence was stolen from red sons and daughters,
By captains ...courageous and sergeant
slaughters.

Inebriated grins and firewater reflections
Whiskey fed rebel's drunken direction
Little big men with guns, eyewitness to
horror.
Tomahawked hopes of forgotten
warriors.

Trails of Tears *(Continued)*

Deafening were screams from
massacred dreams
As souls and spirits came apart at the seams.

Stampeded emotions corralled like cattle
War parties fought but lost the battle

Defeat was swift, the toll was great.
Indian summers cooled by winters of hate.
Their heritage raped, history scalped
by soldiers wearing confederate caps.

Through blinding rain and bitter cold
covered wagon wheel justice took its toll.
As Moccasin grins hid hatred within
Indian burial for next of kin.

No Pinesap dress or witch hazel tea
could heal the wounds on bended knee.
Unable to shield the chill of the night
clinging to life was the ultimate fight.

So one by one red sons, soon fell prey
and lost their lives the American way.
Butchered for fun in the mid day sun.
Where once were rivers, blood now runs?

Their beating drums beat no longer.
Now they march to beats of a
different drummer.
Gone are the sparks in twinkling eyes
chiefs of nothing but pride's bitter reply.

Silhouette

For Marissa P.

Against the shadow of my memory
I saw your figure carved in tear-prints
Molded by fingertips, etched in my mental
With a stroke, so sharp and so deep
I could hardly breathe

Please allow me to be that moment you seek
Because I'm tired of conceding bits of me
Love me, right now, please ....hear my cries

My heart is yours if you'll open your eyes
While looking for me, I've searched for you
Listened for love in skies of blue
Been hoping forever, with each sunset
Waiting for a glimpse of your silhouette

Tell me
Where can I find you, when will I know?
Why must I suffer, needing you so?
Hold me right now, hush don't cry
Because my love is yours if you'll open your eyes.

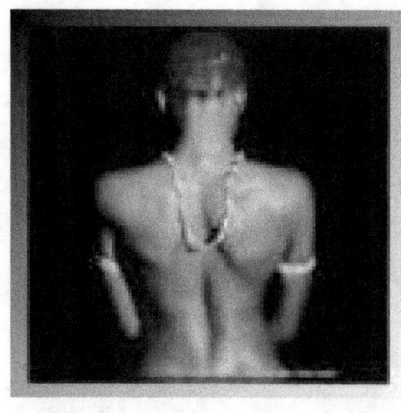

www.ingramcontent.com/pod-product-compliance
Lightning Source LLC
Chambersburg PA
CBHW051436290426
44109CB00016B/1584